61
TRUE STORIES
of
Great
HOAXES & PRANKS

Vikas Khatri

PUSTAK MAHAL®

J-3/16 , Daryaganj, New Delhi-110002
☎ 23276539, 23272783, 23272784 • *Fax:* 011-23260518
E-mail: info@pustakmahal.com • *Website:* www.pustakmahal.com

Sales Centre

- 10-B, Netaji Subhash Marg, Daryaganj, New Delhi-110002
  ☎ 23268292, 23268293, 23279900 • *Fax:* 011-23280567
  E-mail: rapidexdelhi@indiatimes.com
- 6686, Khari Baoli, Delhi-110006
  ☎ 23944314, 23911979

Branches

Bengaluru: ☎ 080-22234025 • *Telefax:* 080-22240209
E-mail: pustak@airtelmail.in • pustak@sancharnet.in
Mumbai: ☎ 022-22010941, 022-22053387
E-mail: rapidex@bom5.vsnl.net.in
Patna: ☎ 0612-3294193 • *Telefax:* 0612-2302719
E-mail: rapidexptn@rediffmail.com
Hyderabad: *Telefax:* 040-24737290
E-mail: pustakmahalhyd@yahoo.co.in

ISBN 978-81-223-1329-1

Edition: 2012

Printed at : Param Offsetters, Okhla, Delhi

Introduction

A hoax is an act of deception which is designed to trick people into believing or doing something. Many hoaxes designed as light-hearted practical jokes have a more serious purpose, and are intended to raise awareness about an issue or to get a community actively involved in something. These uses contrast hoaxes from cons, acts of deception which are perpetrated for financial or personal gain. Many people point out that cons are often harmful, in contrast with hoaxes, which are embarrassing but usually cause no permanent damage.

The word "hoax" has been in the English language since the late 1700s, and it is believed to be derived from hocus, meaning "conjurer". Obviously, people have been perpetrating hoaxes for much longer than this, but the 19th century was so filled with practical jokers and new opportunities for hoaxing that the hoax really blossomed during this period, making it convenient to have a brand new word to describe the phenomenon.

There are different of types of hoaxes, and some involve coordinated effort on the part of people and organizations. For example, a hoax might involve an object which is supposed to do something astounding, and does, when demonstrated by the person perpetrating the hoax. In the modern era, a hoax can be sent in an email; many email hoaxes contain images which are purported to be real but are in fact heavily modified. Typically, once a hoax has been accepted, the people behind the trick unveil the truth.

A traditional time for hoaxing in many countries is the first day of April, also known as April Fools' Day. Practical jokes often abound on this day, and in some regions, governments and news media can get into the fun. The BBC, for example, aired a riveting story in 1957 about the Swiss spaghetti harvest. Hoaxes are also included in graduation festivities at some colleges, with fun-loving graduates playing pranks on each other and the surrounding community.

Some famous events in history such as the moon landing have been called hoaxes by conspiracy theorists, despite ample evidence to the contrary, and some people have suggested that hoaxes can be used for more sinister purposes. For example, a government could hoax its populace into believing that a war was necessary, or a hoax which was designed to raise awareness about a social issue could go too far. Some journalistic hoaxes have also been quite harmful, undermining the reputation of specific newspapers and the journalistic profession in general.

Contents

01 The Lost Tribe - Tasaday

Who are the Tasaday? Depending on whom you ask, you'll hear very different answers to this question. You'll either hear that they're a group of leaf-wearing, stone-age-tool-using cave dwellers who, when they were discovered in 1971 living in a rain forest on the Philippine island of Mindanao, believed they were the only people in the world. Or you'll hear that they're a complete fraud... poor farmers who were cynically coerced into posing as a stone-age tribe by powerful politicians. What's the truth? To that there is no simple answer.

Let's start with the version of the Tasaday story that the world first heard – the one in which they're a real stone-age tribe.

Stone age Tasaday tribe

In this version of events, the Tasaday had been living in their caves in the rain forest for over one thousand years before their isolation ended when a hunter from a neighbouring tribe stumbled upon them while laying his traps. This hunter eventually mentioned their existence to Manuel Elizalde, Jr., the adviser to Ferdinand Marcos on Filipino national minorities, and Elizalde, intrigued, choppered out into the jungle to meet them. (The exact date of this meeting has been reported as either June 4 or 7, 1971). Thus, contact was made.

Soon anthropologists, reporters, and even celebrity visitors such as Charles Lindbergh and Gina Lollobrigida, were flying out to the Tasaday's jungle home. Almost overnight the tribe went from being unknown to being internationally famous. Pictures of them posing in their caves appeared in magazines throughout the world. Documentaries about them aired on TV. A Tasaday child climbing some vines graced the cover of National Geographic. And AP photographer John Nance wrote a bestselling book about them titled *The Gentle Tasaday*.

What most captivated the world about the Tasaday was their peacefulness. It was said they knew no words for enemy or conflict. They seemed to be an uncorrupted version of Man, living in a rain-forest Garden of Eden. Their gentleness was especially striking in 1971 when images of violence and horror were coming daily out of Vietnam.

But there was trouble lurking in the background for the Tasaday, trouble that stemmed from their close association with Manuel Elizalde, Jr. From the moment of their discovery, Elizalde had appointed himself their protector and tightly controlled access to them, but Elizalde was a controversial figure. He was a wealthy playboy with numerous business interests and lofty political ambitions (and thus many enemies), who, despite his jet-setting ways, liked to promote himself as a champion of tribal minorities. The tight rein he kept on access to the Tasaday angered many, and when he persuaded Marcos to declare the Tasaday's rain forest a protected reserve, many were suspicious that sinister motives underlay his interest in the tribe. Specifically, his enemies suspected that he was using the Tasaday both to engineer a massive land-grab and to further his political ambitions.

This was the state of affairs when Marcos declared martial law in 1972, causing access to the Tasaday to become much more restricted. And when Marcos issued a decree in 1976 "protecting the Tasaday and other unexplored cultural communities from unauthorized entry," access to the Tasaday ended altogether. No one was allowed to visit them, and so, from the point of view of the outside world, the Tasaday abruptly vanished from sight.

In 1986 the Marcos government was overthrown, and Oswald Iten, a Swiss journalist, accompanied and guided by a Filipino reporter named Joey Lozano, seized this opportunity to trek out into the jungle to find out what had become of the Tasaday. What Iten found shocked him, and soon became the basis for the second version of the Tasaday story, the one in which they're an outrageous hoax.

Iten found the Tasaday's caves empty and the tribe members living in huts nearby, dressed in jeans and t-shirts, living a simple, but certainly not primitive, lifestyle. Upon questioning them (using Lozano as a translator), two of the Tasaday admitted to Iten that they weren't really a stone-age tribe and never had been. They claimed that Elizalde had pressured them into posing as one. "We didnt live in caves, only near them, until we met Elizalde," they said. "Elizalde forced us to live in the caves so that we'd be better cavemen. Before he came, we lived in huts on the other side of the mountain and we farmed. We took off our clothes because Elizalde told us to do so and promised if we looked poor that we would get assistance. He gave us money to pose as Tasaday and promised us security from counter-insurgency and tribal fighting."

One of the main Tasaday men in 1972 (lower right), and his wife, clearing grass from in front of their house with bush knives (Photo by Oswald Iten)

Iten's discovery sent shockwaves around the world – a fake stone-age tribe managed to surprise even the most jaded newspaper readers – and soon reporters were once again making the journey out into the Filipino rain forest to visit the Tasaday.

Adding an element of sad comedy to the unfolding story, a group of German journalists who arrived within days of Iten's departure found the Tasaday back at their caves dressed in leaves. But upon closer inspection the Germans noticed cloth garments peeking out from beneath the Tasaday's leaves, as if the Tasaday, caught unaware by Iten, had hastily decided to resume the act of being a stone-age tribe, but weren't quite sophisticated enough to pull it off without outside coaching and so had simply pulled on leaves over their clothes.

Researchers, searching for evidence of a hoax, now realized there were many unanswered questions about the Tasaday. For instance, was it really believable that the Tasaday had been isolated for a thousand years given that they lived only a few miles away from a nearby village? Why did the Tasaday seem to be resistant to modern diseases? (Their isolation should have left them with little resistance.) Why had Elizalde so tightly controlled access to the tribe? And why did many of their instruments and utensils appear to have been cut with steel knives if they lacked all knowledge of steel?

Faced with questions like these, and armed with confessions from the Tasaday themselves, the media decided the matter was settled. The Tasaday were dismissed as a hoax, an outrageous publicity stunt dreamed up by Marcos and his cronies to put a gentle face on the country's totalitarian government. This judgement was expressed in documentaries such as Scandal, the Lost Tribe and The Tribe That Never Was. And so the tribe became the laughing stock of the world. Iten dubbed them the Philippine equivalent of a Swiss yodeling society.

However, not everyone thought the matter was settled. The Tasaday still had friends (Elizalde, in particular) who believed in them, and these friends now went to work to repair the tribe's battered reputation.

Despite the overthrow of Marcos, Elizalde continued to wield enough influence in the Philippines to mount a vigorous pro-Tasaday campaign. He led the defense of the Tasaday when the

Philippine Congress investigated the hoax claims in 1987 (the Congress eventually decided the issue was best left to scientists, not politicians, to decide), and in 1988 he flew members of the Tasaday to Manila so that they could file a lawsuit against the Philippine professors who were calling them a hoax. This made the Tasaday the first stone-age tribe to ever sue for libel! These efforts paid off when, also in 1988, Philippine president Corazon Aquino declared that the Tasaday were a "legitimate Stone Age tribe." (It's rumoured that one of Aquino's speechwriters was a personal friend of Elizalde.)

Elizalde could exert political and legal pressure to defend the Tasaday, but these tactics had little effect on scientific opinion. But increasing numbers of scientists were won over to the pro-Tasaday side by the fieldwork of researchers such as Lawrence Reid of the University of Hawaii who lived with the Tasaday for extended periods throughout the 1990s.

Reid studied the Tasaday language and concluded that it was not fake or recently invented. He identified their language as a dialect of Cotabato Manobo (which was not the language spoken by the nearby farming community from which, according to the hoax theory, they had been recruited). However, Reid also concluded that the Tasaday had not been isolated for a thousand years. He speculated that they had splintered off from the Cotabato Manobo community approximately 150 to 200 years ago, perhaps fleeing into the jungle to escape an outbreak of disease.

Reid's linguistic evidence was compelling, but there was one damning piece of evidence that supporters of the Tasaday still had to account for: the Tasaday's own confession that they were a hoax. How to explain this away? This puzzle was answered when two members of the Tasaday admitted that, yes, they had made such a confession, but also insisted that they had been bribed by a translator to make the confession. And why would the translator have done such a thing? Friends of the Tasaday credited this to the anti-Marcos sentiment that ran high in the Philippines in 1986. There were many who were eager to tear down anything associated with Marcos, and since the Tasaday had been considered a showpiece of his regime, a means by which he projected an idyllic view of the Philippines to the outside world, they became a target of choice for Marcos's detractors.

This became the version of the Tasaday story promoted by friends of the Tasaday. The Tasaday, they said, were a real tribe, but they had been the victims of the downfall of Marcos. In other words, the claim that they were a hoax was itself the real hoax! Enemies of Marcos had relentlessly smeared the Tasaday as a way to get back at Marcos. These enemies included loggers who were eager to gain access to the Tasaday rainforest, a desire that had been stymied when Marcos declared it a protected reserve. If the Tasaday were deemed a hoax, the tribe's rights to the reserve would vanish, and the loggers could move in. So, as the friends of the Tasaday explained, there was a powerful financial incentive to make the world believe the Tasaday were a fake stone-age tribe.

So what's a person to conclude? Are the Tasaday a hoax, or is the idea that they're a hoax itself a hoax? Which version of events is correct? The answer is that the truth probably lies somewhere in the middle of all these competing claims.

As Lawrence Reid concluded, the Tasaday really had been living on their own in the rain forest, but apparently only for about 150 years. Not one thousand years. In addition, they seemed to have made contact with neighbouring tribes sometime in the 1950s, and through this contact had acquired steel tools and learned some agricultural skills. So when the wider world discovered them in 1971 they were definitely not as isolated, nor as 'stone-age,' as was first claimed. However, they really were living a very primitive existence.

Elizalde appears guilty of having encouraged the Tasaday to try to look more primitive for the benefit of the cameras. He asked them to wear leaves and hide any steel tools. In this sense, he tweaked the truth, as did the Marcos government which shamelessly promoted the Tasaday as a symbol of the Philippines.

However, the Tasaday themselves appear to have willingly played the role asked of them. After all, they liked the attention and hoped that Elizalde would provide them with aid. So why not do what their new friends wanted them to do? This eagerness to play the part of a stone-age tribe could assume bizarre forms, such as when they donned leaves over their clothes for the benefit of the German reporters in 1986. (The fact that they had been wearing jeans and t-shirts when Iten found them is easily explained by the fifteen years of acculturation they had experienced since 1971.) There was also a surreal moment in 1988 when members of the Tasaday agreed to participate in a cultural festival at Lake Sebu, during which they posed in imitation caves for the benefit of onlookers, like exhibits in a zoo.

Then there's the media, which repeatedly misrepresented the Tasaday. In 1971 it hyped them as a peacenik, utopian, stone-age tribe, and in 1986 it reversed course and branded them an absolute hoax. It could only see the Tasaday in sensationalistic black-and-white terms, as either throwbacks to the stone-age or a fraud, never in shades of grey.

Finally, it does appear that enemies of Marcos and loggers did join forces in the late '80s to discredit the Tasaday, going so far as to bribe members of the group to provide false confessions. So there is some truth to the 'hoax itself is a hoax' claim. In other words, just about everyone involved in the story of the Tasaday was bending the truth for their own purposes. As a result, as Robin Hemley has written, "Nearly every event surrounding the Tasaday is ambiguous and open to interpretation." A very postmodern condition for a stone-age tribe.

To sum up: The Tasaday weren't a true stone-age tribe. But nor were they farmers coerced into playing a stone-age tribe. Instead, they were very poor people living close to Nature in the Philippine jungle who became swept up in and manipulated by global events beyond their control. This version of events isn't as compelling as the versions that made headlines in 1971 and 1986, but it is a good illustration of how the truth is often far messier and more complicated than it appears at first glance.

OO

02 Redheffer's Perpetual Motion Machine

*I*n 1812 a Philadelphia man, Charles Redheffer, claimed to have invented a perpetual motion machine that required no source of energy to run. He built a working model of the machine and applied for funds from the city government to build a larger version. But when inspectors from the city examined it, they realized that Redheffer had simply hidden the power source. To expose Redheffer, they commissioned a local engineer to build a similar machine, and when they showed this to Redheffer he fled

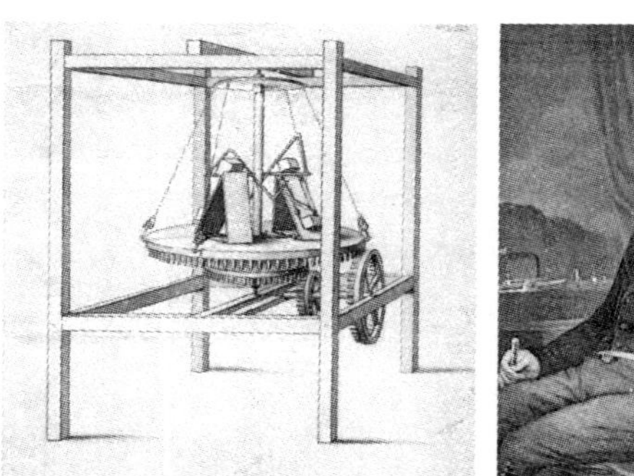

Charles Redheffer and his machine

the city. (This replica is still owned by the Franklin Institute in Philadelphia.)

A year later, Redheffer attempted the same scam in New York City. This time he was exposed by the engineer Robert Fulton who is said to have removed some boards from a wall neighbouring the machine, exposing the source of the machine's power: an old bearded man sitting and eating a crust of bread with one hand, while he turned a hand-crank with the other.

OO

03 The Eruption of Mount Edgecumbe

In 1974 residents of Sitka, Alaska were alarmed when the long-dormant volcano neighbouring them, Mount Edgecumbe, suddenly began to belch out billows of black smoke. People spilled out of their homes onto the streets to gaze up at the volcano, terrified that it was active again and might soon erupt. Luckily it turned out that man, not nature, was responsible for the smoke. A local practical joker named Porky Bickar had flown hundreds of old tires into the volcano's crater and then lit them on fire, all in a (successful) attempt to fool the city dwellers into believing that the volcano was stirring to life. According to local legend, when Mount St. Helens erupted six years later, a Sitka resident wrote to Bickar to tell him, "This time you've gone too far!"

Mount Edgecumbe

OO

04 The Great Stock Exchange Hoax

The Napoleonic wars were a long and trying experience for the British. Therefore, when on February 21, 1814 a man wearing the uniform of a British military officer showed up at an inn on the coast of the English Channel announcing that the war was over, that a party of Cossacks had killed Napoleon, and that the Bourbon government was restored, everyone who heard the news was ecstatic.

Lord Thomas Cochrane

Swift horses were dispatched to speed the news to London. In the capital people rejoiced, and jubilant investors bid up the stocks on the London exchange. Then the bad news arrived. Napoleon was still alive. The report of his death had just been a hoax.

In the investigation that followed, a scheme to manipulate prices on the London stock exchange was uncovered. Some circumstantial evidence indicated that a popular military and political hero called Lord Thomas Cochrane had masterminded the plan. He was arrested, tried, and imprisoned.

But as time passed many began to question whether Cochrane was really guilty, or whether he had been framed by his political enemies. After all, there was no evidence that Cochrane had profited from the stock market's rise. Cochrane escaped from prison and was thrown back inside again before finally being released due to the popular support that he enjoyed. In 1831 the King pardoned him of any involvement in the stock market hoax. Historians now agree that Cochrane was probably not behind the scheme to defraud investors, but the real perpetrator of the hoax remains unknown.

Great Escape

In the 1870s the *New-York Herald* was one of the most widely read and influential papers in the world. It had recently won international acclaim when it financed Henry Stanley's successful quest to find Dr. David Livingstone in the interior of Africa. But it followed up this success with a stunt that was almost as widely denounced.

On November 9, 1874 the Herald published a front-page article claiming that the animals had escaped from their cages in the Central Park Zoo and were rampaging through the city. A lion had been seen inside a church. A rhinoceros had fallen into a sewer. The police and national guard were heroically battling the beasts, but already forty-nine people were dead and two hundred injured. It was "a bloody and fearful carnival," the article despaired. And the animals were still on the loose!

Central Park zoo animal escape

Many readers panicked when they read the article. However, those who did so hadn't read to the end where it stated (in rather small print) that, "the entire story given above is a pure fabrication."

Along with the Great Moon Hoax of 1835, the New York Zoo Escape ranks as one of the most notorious media hoaxes of the nineteenth century.

Thomas Connery, an editor at the Herald, later confessed in an article published in *Harper's Weekly* in 1893, that the idea for the hoax had been his. He insisted that James Gordon Bennett, Jr., the owner of the Herald, had not been responsible for it, although many assumed Bennett must have, at least, given it his approval.

Connery claimed that the idea for the hoax came to him after he witnessed a leopard almost escape while being transferred from an animal-carriage into its cage in the Central Park Zoo (referred to as the "menagerie" at the time). Wishing to call attention to the conditions at the zoo, Connery first thought of writing a column scolding the zoo keepers, but then decided that something more attention-grabbing was needed. He conceived of the idea of "a harmless little hoax, with just enough semblance of reality to give a salutary warning."

He first assigned the writing of the article to Harry O'Connor, but he felt that O'Connor's resulting piece was too obviously a "transparent imposition." Therefore, he reassigned the article to Joseph Clarke, who wrote the version that ran on November 9. The article ran to over 10,000 words in length, and occupied six full columns. It appeared on page three, which was considered to be the front page. (The first two pages were always filled with ads and acted as a cover page for the paper.) "AWFUL CALAMITY," the headline screamed. "A Shocking Sabbath Carnival of Death."

The article began by offering general details of what it said had been a day of horror, beginning Sunday afternoon and continuing through Monday morning (November 9), when the article appeared. Because wild animals were supposedly still on the loose, it noted that the mayor had issued a proclamation urging all citizens "to keep within their houses or residences until the wild animals now at large are captured or killed."

The tragedy was said to have begun after a reckless keeper provoked a rhinoceros by prodding it with a stick through the bars. The enraged beast smashed down its cage, thereby escaping and killing its keepers. In its rage, it then battered down the cages of the other animals, who proceeded to scatter throughout the city, wreaking havoc wherever they went.

The text did not shy away from offering up all the gruesome details of the animal attacks:

Backing down from the mangled body with a swiftness almost incredible from his bulk, the rhinoceros plunged his horrid horn into the dead keeper...

The panther was crouched over Hyland's body, gnawing horribly at his head. I recognized his body by the striped shirt which I could just see hanging tattered from the arm...

Men and women rushed in all directions away from the beast, who sprang upon the shoulders of an aged lady, burying his fangs in her neck and carrying her to the ground.

Scenes of increasing strangeness were described: a lion and a tiger fighting on fifty-ninth street, a battle between a sea lion and a rhinoceros, an anaconda attempting to eat a giraffe, Swedish hunters stalking a lioness on Broadway, a Bengal Tiger shot on Madison Avenue, a panther attacking worshipers inside a church on West Fifty-third Street, and carnage as a tiger leapt on board a ferryboat.

Specific names were given. A list of the dead and wounded was offered. And bolded column sub-headers highlighted all the most salient points: THE WILD ANIMALS ARE LOOSE, POLICE ARMED WITH REVOLVERS, CIRCLE OF FEAR-STRICKEN PEOPLE, CONFUSION AND DESTRUCTION.

Only if a reader read carefully to the end, would he have found the truth revealed in the final paragraph:

Of course the entire story given above is a pure fabrication. Not one word of it is true. Not a single act or incident described has taken place. It is a huge hoax, a wild romance, or whatever other epithet of utter untrustworthiness our readers may choose to apply to it. It is simply a fancy picture which crowded upon the mind of the writer a few days ago while he was gazing through the iron bars of the cages of the wild animals in the menagerie at Central Park.

By all accounts, the article caused widespread panic throughout the city. Armed men rushed into the streets, ready to defend their homes. Reporters were dispatched to cover the story. The police mobilized. Parents rushed to bring their children back from school.

Recalling the reaction nineteen years later, Connery wrote: "while in the hoax General John A. Dix was represented as shooting the Bengal tiger, in reality he did sally forth on the morning of the publication armed with a rifle, firmly believing that the Herald's story was true, and that danger might lurk at any corner."

Connery also claimed that the editor of the *New York Times* ran out of his home waving two pistols in the air, ready to shoot the first animal he encountered.

Rival papers throughout the United States quickly and unanimously denounced the hoax. *The New-York Times,* while admitting that the "animals in the Central Park are confined in the flimsiest cages ever seen," described the article as an "intensely stupid and unfeeling hoax" and printed letters from readers claiming to have been terrified by the story. It commented sarcastically that if "charming sketches of dead children and dying old ladies do not move the reader to roars of laughter, his sense of fun must be somewhat different from that with which the proprietor or editor of the *New-York Herald* has been endowed."

The Galveston Daily News wrote: "To be in keeping with its enterprise, the Herald should bribe a keeper to let loose a lion or two upon occasion, so as to bring up that journal's prophetic record... Bennett had better recall Stanley from the interior of Africa. He is the crack lion shot of the Herald establishment, and should be at home to protect it."

The New York Times also reported that a group of citizens paid a visit to the District Attorney's office to express their outrage at the Herald's hoax and to find out whether the paper could be indicted on account of it. The District Attorney promised to give it his attention. However, no charges were ever brought against the paper.

For its part, the Herald feigned surprise when the article provoked such an enormous reaction, but it was wholly unrepentant. By way of apology, it simply inserted a short article into the next issue, titled "Wild Beasts," urging that safety precautions at the zoo be improved. Understandably, the public was underwhelmed by this show of contrition. However, the Herald did not report any drop in circulation as a result of the hoax.

According to rumour, the Herald's wild animal hoax had an impact far beyond the controversy it temporarily stirred up. It may have been the inspiration for the elephant that serves as the symbol of the Republican party.

The link connecting the Herald's hoax to the adoption of the elephant as the republican party symbol was the political cartoonist Thomas Nast.

In 1874 the Herald was frequently editorializing against President Grant (a Republican), warning voters that he planned to seek a third term in office, despite the tradition, started by George Washington, that Presidents should limit themselves to two terms. The Herald charged Grant with "Caesarism." Republicans insisted that these charges were false.

The story goes that, in the week following the wild animal hoax, Nast (at the time a staunch Republican) published an illustration in *Harper's Weekly* in which he satirized both the hoax and the Herald's attempts to scare voters about Grant's intentions. The illustration showed the Herald as a jackass, disguised in the skin of a lion tagged "Caesarism." The appearance of the Herald was scaring zoo animals who were running frightened through the woods of Central Park. One of the animals was an elephant labeled "The Republican Vote." The cartoon was captioned "The Third-Term Panic."

A few weeks later Nast returned to this theme, with a cartoon that showed the Republican Vote (again represented as an elephant) falling into a pit with a variety of other animals. The caption read, "Caught in a trap – the result of the third-term hoax." The reference to the third-term hoax was a pun, alluding simultaneously to the Herald's charges of "Caesarism" and its recent wild-animal hoax.

Other cartoonists, inspired by Nast's cartoon, also began to use an elephant to represent Republicans, and so the symbol stuck. By the 1880s it was firmly established as the symbol of the party.

The link between the Democratic party and an ass (or donkey) traced further back, to the time of Andrew Jackson. But Nast's cartoons also helped to popularize that symbol.

This story of the origin of the Republican party symbol has been frequently repeated. For instance, William Safire tells it in his book *New Language of Politics* (1972).

For the most part, it is true. Nast did publish these cartoons, and they did popularize the association of republicans with elephants. But the story is incorrect in one key detail. Nast's first cartoon (the one titled "The Third-Term Panic) was published a week before the wild animal hoax, not after it. Therefore, the cartoon could not have been inspired by the hoax. In fact, some suggest the opposite is true – that the hoax itself was inspired by Nast's illustration. This seems possible, but no one at the Herald ever commented on whether Nast's illustration served as a source of inspiration for them.

The Cottingley Fairies

Nine-year-old Frances Griffiths was in trouble. She had been playing down near the stream called Cottingley beck and had slipped on wet stepping stones, falling into the water soaking her shoes and stockings. Her mother would not be pleased. Especially since her mother had told Frances to stay away from the stream.

In that year, 1917, Frances Griffiths had just arrived in England from South Africa and she and her mother were staying with Frances's aunt. Frances and her cousin, sixteen-year-old Elsie Wright, often played together near the beck to the annoyance of their mothers.

When Frances returned from the stream that day with wet feet, her mother persisted in asking her why she constantly returned to that forbidden place. The girl's answer precipitated a strange affair that lasted nearly 70 years and involved one of the greatest literary minds of the day. She told her mother she went to see the fairies.

Her mother and aunt greeted this statement with disbelief. Frances's cousin Elsie added that she had seen the fairies too, and suggested to Frances that they borrow Mr. Wright's camera and take some photographs of them. Within a half hour of taking the camera, they were back begging Elsie's father to develop the film plates for them. After tea, Mr. Wright (with Elsie at this side) developed the film in his darkroom. He was astonished when the picture showed Frances looking straight at the camera while a group of five fairies danced before her on an earthen bank.

After the initial surprise, Mr. Wright dismissed the fairies as cardboard cutouts. He knew his daughter was a talented artist who enjoyed drawing fairy figures. Eventually Mr. Wright stopped loaning his camera to his daughter and niece after they took another photo with Elsie posed next to what appeared to be a gnome.

Frances with Cottingley Fairies

Except for a few copies of the pictures given to friends and family the whole matter might have stayed a private affair. In 1919 the mothers Polly Wright and Annie Griffiths attended a meeting about Theosophy. Theosophy was a philosophy that included in its teaching the possibility of nature spirits. After the meeting was over the women approached the speaker about the pictures. This brought the photographs to the attention of Edward Gardner, a well-known leader in the Theosophical movement. He wrote to Polly Wright telling her that the photographs were "the best of its kind I should think anywhere." Gardner obtained from the Wrights the original negative glass plates and sent them to photographic expert Harold Snelling. It was said of Snelling, "What Snelling doesn't know about faked photography isn't worth knowing."

After examing them Snelling concluded, "This plate is a single exposure. These dancing figures are not made of paper nor any fabric; they are not painted on a photographic background-but what gets me most is that all these figures have moved during the exposure."

What Snelling meant by his last sentence was that the camera's shutter speed must have been set very low (something that can be confirmed by the movement of the blurred waterfall behind Frances in the first picture) and that the fairies appeared to be blurred as if the exposure had caught them moving in their dance.

Gardner showed the pictures to his cousin, who in turn brought them to the attention of Sir Arthur Conan Doyle. Conan Doyle was author of the *Sherlock Holmes* stories as well as several novels including *The Lost World*.

Conan Doyle was a member of the Spiritualist movement and believed that the living could communicate with the dead through psychics and seances. He was very open to the idea of fairies and welcomed the photos as evidence of a world beyond physical reality. Conan Doyle considered going to Bradford himself to interview the family, but was too busy preparing for a trip to Australia. He asked Gardner to go instead.

After talking to the girls, Gardner reported to Conan Doyle that he believed they were telling the truth. Conan Doyle then used the pictures in a story he was writing about fairies for *The Strand* magazine and suggested that more photographs be taken while the girls were being observed by a "disinterested witness."

The article received much criticism. Major Edward Halls, a radium expert, wrote:

"On the evidence I have no hesitation in saying that these photographs could have been faked. I criticize the attitude of those who declare there is something supernatural in the circumstances attending to the taking of these pictures because, as a medical man, I believe that the inculcation of such absurd ideas into the minds of children will result in later life in manifestations and nervous disorder and mental disturbances..."

In 1920 Edward Gardner returned to Bradford with a new camera and persuaded the girls to try to get some more fairy pictures. In a few weeks they had taken several additional photographs with fairies in them. This made a total of five.

In 1921 a well-known clairvoyant, Geoffrey Hodson ,was brought to Cottingley to see if he could detect the spirits. He claimed that he, like the girls, could see them.

For many years the debate continued as to whether the girls had actually captured fairies on film. Meanwhile the world lost track of Elsie and Frances. In 1966 Peter Chambers of the *Daily Express* decided to do a follow-up on the stories and located Elsie. She told him in an interview that the fairies might have been "figments of my imagination," but it was unclear if she meant that she had indeed faked the photographs or somehow believed she had photographed her thoughts.

Five years later the BBC-TV program Nationwide approached Elsie for another interview. Elsie seemed very evasive on whether she had actually photographed real fairies and the BBC crew came to the conclusion that the pictures had been paper cutouts made to stand up with hat pins.

Finally in 1981 and 1982 Joe Cooper interviewed Frances and Elsie for an article in The Unexplained. Elsie admitted that all five of the photographs had been faked. Frances claimed that the first four had been faked, but the fifth was real. Both ladies contended they had indeed seen real fairies near the beck.

The hoax had been carried out by using the cutout and hatpin method as many people had suspected. Elsie had some art training and drew the characters based on drawings by Arthur Shepperson in Princess Mary's Gift Book of which Frances owned a copy. Using a sharp pair of scissors owned by Frances's mother, they cut them out and secured them to a bank of earth with hat pins. After the photographs were taken, they dropped the evidence into the stream and brought the camera back to Elsie's father so that he could develop the pictures. Though some had suspected Mr. Wright of being in on the hoax, the girls deny he knew anything about it.

Looking at the photographs now, it seems amazing anyone could not see that the figures are one-dimensional cardboard or paper cutouts. In a careful examination of the gnome picture, it is possible to see where the pin passes through the paper. Elsie herself in 1982 expressed surprise that so many people were fooled by what seemed to her an obvious fake. Still, we must remember that photography was a new art then and people were not as experienced in seeing photographs as we are today. Also the images were cleaned up and sharpened for their publication in *The Strand*. Finally, perhaps we can excuse some of Conan Doyle's gullibility in accepting the images remembering that he had a photographic expert (Snelling) examine the pictures and state they were not fakes. What excuse Snelling might have had is hard to imagine..

The story of the Cottingley Fairies was put to film in 1997 under the title *Photographing Fairies*.

Perhaps the whole affair can best be summed up by a quote from a columnist in the newspaper Truth on the Conan Doyle's Strand article.

"For the true explanation of these fairy photographs what is wanted is not a knowledge of occult phenomena, but a knowledge of children."

07 The Calaveras Skull

On February 25, 1866, workers found a human skull buried deep inside a mine on Bald Mountain in Calaveras County, California. The skull was located 130 feet below the surface, beneath a layer of lava. The owner of the mine, James Mattison, gave the skull to a merchant who in turn passed it on to a local physician until it eventually found its way into the possession of J.D. Whitney, the State Geologist of California and Professor of Geology at Harvard University. Whitney determined that the skull belonged to a Pliocene age man. This made it the oldest known record of human existence in North America. It also suggested that humans had lived in the Americas far longer than previously thought, perhaps as long as they had lived in Europe.

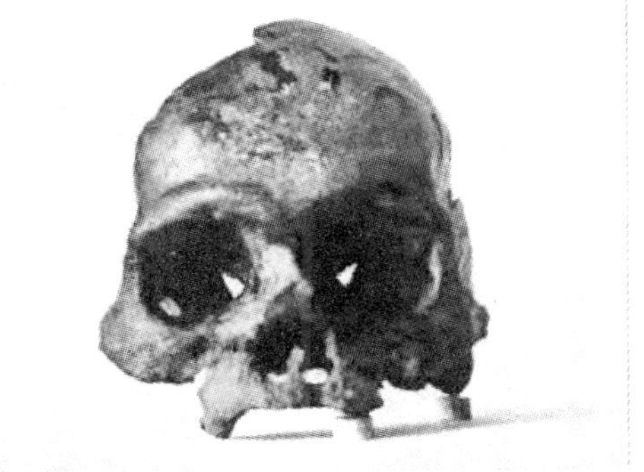

Calveras Skull

However, the authenticity of the skull was challenged by other scholars. What ensued was a long controversy between those who insisted the skull had been planted at the mine, and those who insisted it was a genuine find.

It took many years before the skull was decisively determined to be a fake. The skull was simply too modern in character to be from the Pliocene age. In addition, the sediment attached to it was not from the mine deposit, indicating it had been planted. The skull was probably planted by miners playing a practical joke.

As early as 1869, a San Francisco newspaper declared, "We believe the whole story worthy of no scientific credence... a minister... told us that the miners freely told him that they purposely got up the whole affair as a joke on Professor Whitney."

Smithsonian scientist W.H. Holmes pointed out that the sediment found with the skull was of a modern type. The skull itself also looked modern. In addition, many scientists were disturbed by the fact that a qualified researcher had not had a chance to examine the skull in situ.

Despite the doubts expressed about the skull, Whitney continued to believe it was genuine. He was eventually replaced at Harvard by F.W. Putnam, who also argued for the skull's authenticity.

By the 1890s the skull was still accepted as genuine by the academic community, but it was becoming obvious that it did not fit into the growing fossil record of man's evolution. So in 1901 Putnam decided to determine, once and for all, whether the skull was authentic.

While in California he did some research and learned that in 1865 a number of Indian skulls had been dug up from a nearby Indian burial site. One of these skulls had been planted in the Bald Mountain mine so that workers would later find it. Despite hearing this story, Putnam was still not ready to declare the skull a fake. Instead he simply conceded that "It may be impossible ever to determine to the satisfaction of the archaeologist the place where the skull was actually found."

To confuse the matter, a careful comparison of the skull with descriptions of the skull at the time it had originally been found, led investigators to conclude that the two were not the same. In other words, at some point between the time that it had been dug up and the time that it had come into the possession of Whitney, the skull had been switched.

It now seems clear that neither the skull found in the mine, nor the skull acquired by Whitney, were genuine ancient skulls. The skulls were simply too modern in character to be from the Pliocene age, and in addition, the sediment attached to them was not from the mine deposit, indicating that they had been planted.

Historian Ralph Dexter concludes, "The desire on the part of miners to play a practical joke, the anxiety of archaeologists to prove the existence of early humankind in North America, the firm convictions and good faith of those involved in an honest mistake, and the confusion resulting from a mix up of skulls, led to this long drawn-out controversy, unique in the annals of American archaeology."

Pope Joan or ?

According to legend, Pope Joan was a woman who concealed her gender and ruled as pope for two years, from 853-855 AD. Her identity was exposed when, riding one day from St. Peter's to the Lateran, she stopped by the side of the road and, to the astonishment of everyone, gave birth to a child.

The legend is unconfirmed. Skeptics note that the first references to Pope Joan only appear hundreds of years after her supposed reign. However, supporters argue that the Church may have attempted to erase all evidence of her existence from the historical record.

Pope John VIII

Pope Joan was said to have been born an Englishwoman. She concealed her gender to pursue her scholarly ambitions – the life of a scholar not being allowed to a woman at that time. Calling herself John Anglicus, she travelled to Athens where she gained a reputation for her knowledge of the sciences. Eventually she came to lecture at the Trivium in Rome where her fame grew even larger. Still disguised as a man, she became a Cardinal, and when Pope Leo IV died in 853 AD was unanimously elected pope.

As Pope John VIII she ruled for two years. However, while riding one day from St. Peter's to the Lateran, she had to stop by the side of the road and supposedly gave birth to a child. According to one legend, upon discovering the Pope's true gender, the people of Rome tied her feet together and dragged her behind a horse while stoning her, until she died. Another legend has it that she was sent to a faraway convent to repent her sins and that the child she bore grew up to become the Bishop of Ostia.

It is not known whether the story of Pope Joan is true. The first known reference to her occurs in the thirteenth century, 350 years after her supposed reign. Around this time her image also began to appear as the High Priestess card in the Tarot deck.

The Catholic Church at first seemed to accept the reality of Pope Joan. Marginal notes in a fifteenth century document refer to a statue called "The Woman Pope with Her Child" that was supposedly erected near the Lateran. There was also a rumour that, as a result of Pope Joan, for many years the chairs used during papal consecrations had holes in their seats, so that an official check of the pope's gender could be performed.

During the Reformation in the sixteenth century, the Catholic Church began to deny the existence of Pope Joan. However, at the same time, Protestant writers insisted on her reality, primarily because the existence of a female pope was a convenient piece of anti-Catholic propaganda.

Modern scholars disagree about the historicity of Pope Joan.

The Predictions of Isaac Bickerstaff

*I*n February 1708 a previously unknown London astrologer named Isaac Bickerstaff published an almanac in which he predicted the death by fever of the famous rival astrologer John Partridge. According to Bickerstaff, Partridge would die on March 29 of that year. Partridge indignantly denied the prediction, but on March 30 Bickerstaff released a pamphlet announcing that he had been correct: Partridge was dead. It took a day for the news to settle in, but soon everyone had heard of the astrologer's demise. On April 1, April Fool's Day, Partridge was woken by a sexton outside his window who wanted to know if there were any orders for his funeral sermon. Then, as Partridge walked down the street, people stared at him as if they were looking at a ghost or stopped to tell him that he looked exactly like someone they knew who was dead. As hard as he tried, Partridge couldn't convince people that he wasn't dead. Bickerstaff, it turned out, was a pseudonym for the great satirist Jonathan Swift. His prognosticatory practical joke upon Partridge worked so well that the astrologer finally was forced to stop publishing his almanacs, because he couldn't shake his reputation as the man whose death had been foretold.

Isaac Bickerstaff

OO

The Donation of Constantine

The Donation of Constantine was a document supposedly written by Emperor Constantine (285-337 A.D.) granting the Catholic Church ownership of vast territories within the western Roman Empire. The document stated that he made this generous gift out of gratitude to Pope Sylvester I who had converted him to Christianity and had cured him of leprosy. For centuries the Donation legitimated the Church's possession of the papal lands in Italy. Unfortunately, the Donation was entirely fake, as even the Church eventually acknowledged.

Constantine

The truth is that the Church only officially acquired the papal lands in 756 A.D. when King Pepin of the Frankish Empire gave them to the Church as a gift. 756 A.D. also appears to be the time when the text of the Donation first appeared. It was probably created by a cleric either in Rome or the Frankish court. Its purpose may have been to allow the King to claim that he was returning, not giving, the papal lands to the Church. In this way, the fiction of the Donation added legitimacy to a convenient political marriage between the Catholic Church and the Frankish state.

The Donation was not revealed to be a forgery until 1440. In that year Lorenzo Valla published his Discourse on the Forgery of the Alleged Donation of Constantine, in which he enumerated the large number of historical anachronisms that pervaded the work. For instance, it referred to Byzantia as a province when in the fourth century it was only a city, it referred to temples in Rome that did not yet exist, and it referred to 'Judea' even though in Constantine's time the Romans referred to this territory as 'Palestina.' Valla could have added that emperor Constantine never had leprosy, making it impossible for Pope Sylvester to have cured him of this disease. The Catholic Church suppressed Valla's work for years. Centuries later, it publicly conceded that the Donation was a fake.

The Catholic Church ceded the Papal States back to Italy in 1929.

The Holy Foreskin Mystery

Of all the holy relics that circulated throughout medieval Europe, relics associated with Jesus Christ – anything he supposedly touched or used during his life – were the most prized. By this measure, no relic was more valuable than the Holy Foreskin since it was an actual body part of Christ. In fact, the foreskin is the only body part the Bible specifically mentions being removed from Christ during his life (eight days after his birth) and which presumably stayed behind on Earth after he ascended into Heaven.

The Holy Foreskin of Christ first made an appearance in medieval Europe around 800 AD, when King Charlemagne presented it as a gift to Pope Leo III. Charlemagne said it had been given to him by an angel.

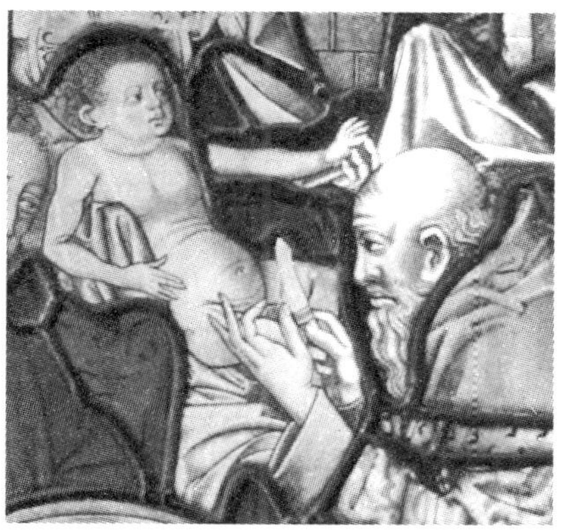

Circumcision of Christ

However, rival foreskins soon began to pop up all over Europe. All told, twenty-one different churches claimed to have the Holy Foreskin, often at the same time. Various miraculous powers were attributed to these foreskins. In particular, they were supposed to be able to protect women during childbirth.

Given the glut of Holy Foreskins, churches made efforts to have their foreskin authenticated by Church leaders as the sole genuine article. In the early 12th century, the monks of San Giovanni in

Laterano, Rome asked Pope Innocent III to rule on the authenticity of their foreskin, but he declined to do so. Later, the monks of Charroux claimed their foreskin to be the only real one, pointing out that it apparently yielded drops of blood. This convinced Pope Clement VII (1523-1534) who declared theirs to be the authentic thing.

However, the Church eventually sought to extract itself from the Holy Foreskin controversy and adopted the view that all the rival foreskins were frauds. In 1900 it made it a crime punishable by excommunication to write or speak about the Holy Foreskin.

Some medieval theologians argued that all the Holy Foreskins necessarily had to be frauds since the actual Holy Foreskin had, they asserted, ascended into Heaven with Christ. The 17th century theologian Leo Allatius speculated in his essay De Praeputio Domini Nostri Jesu Christi Diatriba that the holy foreskin had ascended into heaven at the same time as Jesus, and had become the rings of Saturn.

OO

12 Devils Tower Treasure

Near the northeast corner of Wyoming is a striking mountain of igneous rock that looks like a gigantic tree-stump. A tree stump over a thousand feet high. Columns run vertically up the top part of the rock like giant scratches. The name given to the mountain by the white man was "Devils Tower." The Indians had many names for it. One of them was "Bear Lodge."

Because it is so unusual in its appearance the tower has figured into many Native American legends and in 1977 it was used as the location for the finale of Steven Speilberg's film *Close Encounters of the Third Kind.*

Devils Tower

Perhaps the most widely-known legend the Native Americans had about the tower was told by the Kiowa: There were seven girls playing near their village when they were chased by some bears. The girls jumped on a low rock and called to it "Rock, take pity on us, rock save us!" The rock heard them and grew up towards the sky. The bears jumped at the rock scratching it, but they could not climb it. The rock took the girls so high that they became stars. A constellation we now call the Plediades.

There is one story, though, that does not deal with the creation of the rock but what is below it. Years ago a resident of that part northeast Wyoming visited Yankton, South Dakota. While there, he showed a picture of Devils Tower to some elderly Sioux Indians he met. One of them got very excited when he saw the picture.

"Has a passageway been found at the base of the tower?" he asked.

When the resident replied no, the man seemed disappointed. With a little urging, the resident was able to get the Indian to pass on to him the legend about the tower that he had been told. It went something like this:

Many years before three braves had been hunting near the tower. While exploring the rocks at the base of the mountain, they discovered a passageway underneath it. They made torches out of pitch pine knots for light and started exploring the tunnel. They found the passage strewn with bones. Perhaps human bones. At the end, the tunnel opened up into a cave with an underground lake some 25 yards long and more than 15 yards wide. Around the lake were large quantities of gold.

The braves were not prepared to take the gold with them, so they left the tunnel and hid the entrance so that others would not find it. They intended to return to get the gold at a later time, but never did. One of the braves, on his deathbed, told the story to other members of his tribe and the tale had been handed down for several generations before reaching the old Indian.

So is there a cave with gold under Devil's tower? Nobody has ever found one. Also the geology of the mountain, an igneous intrusion, does not seem to make it a promising location to find caves directly under the mountain. The tale sounds very much like other "lost mine" stories of the Old West, like the story of the "lost Dutchman" mine and Beale's mine, which seem to have little factual basis.

On the other hand, the Black Hills area in which the tower is located, has some of the largest caves in the world underneath it, including Wind Cave and Jewel Cave. The Black Hills area is also known for gold mining that inspired a major gold rush in the 1880's. So maybe, like many legends, there is some truth to the Devil's Tower story. Perhaps the lost cavern is not underneath the tower, but nearby, waiting for someone to find it.

OO

13 The Letter of Prester John

*I*n the mid-twelfth century, at a time when European rulers felt threatened by the growing power of Muslim nations on their borders, a letter suddenly appeared from Prester John, who described himself as a Christian king of great wealth living in the far east. The letter was addressed to the Byzantine emperor Manuel Comnenus.

Prester John claimed to be a descendant of one of the Three Magi. He wrote that his kingdom stretched from India to the land where the sun rises, and that it was inhabited by fantastic creatures such as seven-horned bulls, birds so large they could lift and kill an armoured man, and horned men with three eyes in the back of their heads. He even claimed there was a fountain of perpetual youth in his kingdom.

The Letter of Prester John

The letter circulated throughout all the European courts. In 1177, Pope Alexander III instructed his personal envoy to travel east, search for Prester John, and deliver a reply to his letter. It was hoped Prester John would come to the aid of the Christian nations in Europe, but no response ever came. Nevertheless, European explorers continued to search for the mythical king for centuries.

The true author of the letter remains unknown. Whoever it was, he was familiar with old legends, which he borrowed heavily from – legends such as the tales of Alexander the Great's adventures in the East. Linguistic evidence suggests the letter originated in Italy. The author probably intended to offer hope to the Christian armies fighting the crusades, and in this respect he succeeded, even though the hope was a false one.

OO

14 The Travels of Marco Polo – Silk Route?

Marco Polo's famous Description of the World was written around 1298. It was Polo's account of the many years he had spent in China.

Marco Polo

According to the book's prologue, Marco Polo first travelled to China in 1271 with his father and uncle who were both merchants. While in China, he met the great ruler, Qubilai Khan, and so impressed him that Khan made Marco his special emissary, sending him on missions throughout the various far-flung provinces of China. Marco Polo finally returned to Venice with his family in 1295. He wrote the account of his travels in 1298 while imprisoned in Genoa (or rather, he described his travels to a French writer named Rustichello who wrote the actual book for him).

Marco Polo's book became enormously influential and served in Europe as one of the primary sources of information about the Orient for many centuries. Christopher Columbus, for instance, took the book with him on his fateful voyage to the Americas. It also inspired a number of legends, such as the idea that Marco Polo brought the secrets of spaghetti and ice cream with him back from China (he didn't).

Some scholars now suspect, however, that Marco Polo never went to China. The argument for this case has been laid out by Frances Wood in her book *Did Marco Polo Go to China?*

The basic argument against Marco Polo involves a set of telling omissions. First of all, no reference has ever been found in Chinese archives to an Italian visitor like Marco Polo, despite the fact that China's bureaucrats kept numerous forms of documentation and recorded the presence of many other westerners. If Marco Polo really did serve as a special emissary to the Great Khan, it seems unusual that his presence would never have been noted.

Second of all, Polo's account omits many details about Chinese culture that seemed very important to almost all later European travellers. For instance, Wood notes Polo's "apparent failure to pick up even a few Chinese or Mongol place-names in his seventeen-year stay in China." Nor does he ever mention the Chinese style of writing, despite the dramatic difference between Chinese script and the Roman alphabet.

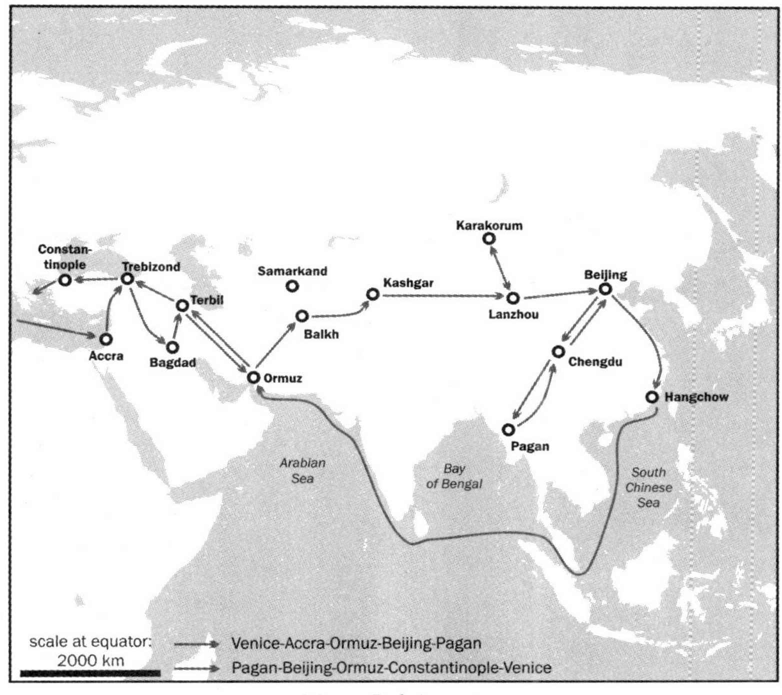

Marco Polo's route

Marco Polo does not mention seeing woodblock printing, which was then unknown in Europe. He never mentions the Chinese custom of drinking tea (also unknown in Europe at that time), despite the fact that he discusses varieties of Chinese wine. He never mentions the practice of foot-binding, even though this custom fascinated all other Europeans who travelled to China. He never mentions the use of chopsticks; and finally, he fails to mention the Great Wall of China.

Marco Polo did, however, identify some important features of Chinese society. For instance, he described porcelain, the use of coal, and the use of paper money—all unknown to Europeans in the thirteenth century. Nevertheless, it is still hard to imagine that someone could actually go to China and manage to miss all the details that he missed.

Wood suggests that Marco Polo probably never travelled further than his family's trading posts on the Black Sea, but that he had access to Persian or Arabic guidebooks to China from which he was able to piece together his account of China. He probably wrote his account in response to a growing demand for geographies during the late thirteenth century.

Kremvax

*I*n 1984, back in the Stone Age of the internet, a message was distributed to the members of Usenet (the online messaging community that was one of the first forms the internet took) announcing that the Soviet Union was joining Usenet. This was quite a shock to many, since most assumed that cold war security concerns would have prevented such a link-up. The message purported to come from Konstantin Chernenko (from the address chernenko@kremvax.UUCP) who explained that the Soviet Union wanted to join the network in order to "have a means of having an open discussion forum with the American and European people." The message created a flood of responses. Two weeks later its true author, a European man named Piet Beertema, revealed that it was a hoax. This is believed to be the first hoax on the internet. Six years later, when Moscow really did link up to the internet, it adopted the domain name 'kremvax' in honour of the hoax.

Piet Beertema

The Shroud of Turin

The Shroud of Turin first came to the attention of the public in 1355, when it was exhibited at the Church of St. Mary in Lirey, France. It had been given to the church by a French knight, Geoffroy de Charny, who probably acquired it in Constantinople.

Its supporters claim that this fourteen-foot piece of cloth bearing the image of a naked man was the funeral shroud of Christ. They argue that only supernatural means could have created such an image.

Skeptics dismiss the shroud as a medieval forgery, arguing that: 1) there was a flourishing trade in false relics during the middle ages; 2) a medieval forger could definitely have created such an image (researchers have offered a variety of theories to explain how it might have been done); and 3) the man's body is oddly proportioned (his head is too large), which suggests the image is a painting.

Throughout its history, the shroud has been a subject of controversy. Soon after it was discovered, a report to Pope Clement argued that the shroud was merely a painting, and that it was being falsely displayed as a true relic in order to solicit donations to the church. As a consequence, Pope Clement declared the relic a fraud.

In 1453 the shroud was acquired by de Charny's granddaughter who eventually sold it to the Duke of Savoy. The Savoys exhibited it for many decades, claiming that it was the holy shroud that had covered Christ as he lay in the tomb. In 1532 it was almost destroyed in a fire. The shroud still displays burn marks from this incident.

Throughout the twentieth century researchers dueled back and forth over the shroud's authenticity. In 1982 a group calling itself

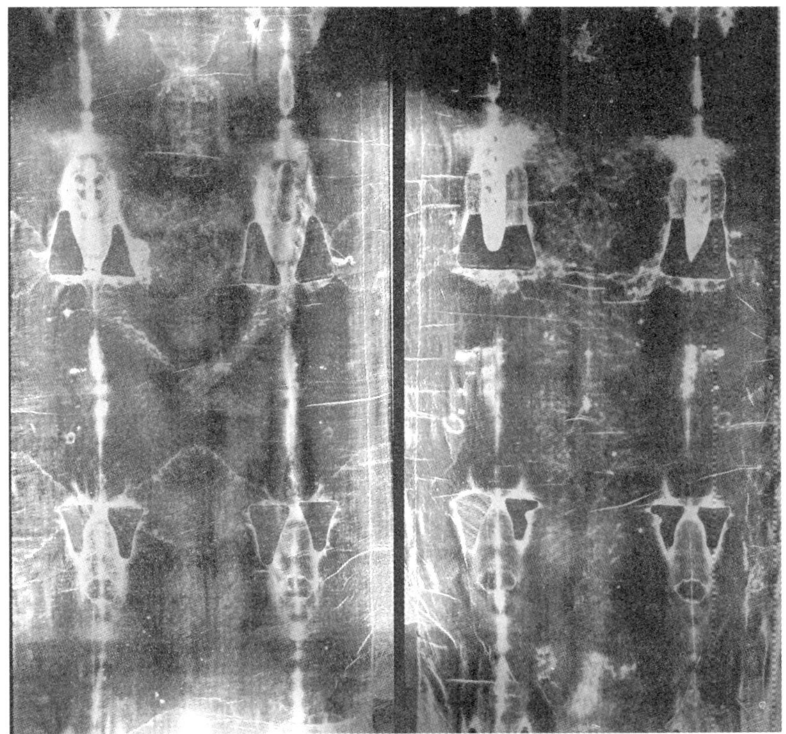

Full length negatives of the shroud of Turin

the Shroud of Turin Research Project declared it to be genuine after studying samples lifted from the cloth using tape. However, radiocarbon tests performed later during the 1980s dated the shroud to approximately the fourteenth century, indicating that the relic was a fake. Nevertheless, shroud supporters found many reasons to dispute the radiocarbon testing, and so the debate raged on and likely will for the foreseeable future.

Recent News About the Shroud

Aug 22, 2002: The Vatican admitted it had secretly been allowing a scientist to perform tests on the shroud for the past few months. The scientist was trying to get a more accurate reading of the exact age of the shroud's fibers, following criticism of 1988 tests of the age of the fibers.

Apr 18, 2004: A second face was discovered on the backside of the shroud.

January 31, 2005: New tests suggested that the shroud may be older than previously thought. Tests done in 1988 had apparently (mistakenly) analyzed patches woven into the shroud following the fire in 1532. Raymond Rogers has published a paper in Thermochimica Acta stating that the shroud itself appears to be far older, between 1,300 and 3,000 years old.

March 2005: Nathan Wilson published an article suggesting that the shroud could have easily been created by a medieval forger if the forger painted a figure of a man on a piece of glass, placed the glass over a linen shroud, and left this setup out in the sun for a couple of days. The sun would bleach the linen, but leave behind a photo-negative image of the figure painted on the glass.

17 The Greatest Liar of all Time - Sir John Mandeville

The seventeenth-century writer Sir Thomas Browne declared that Sir John Mandeville was "the greatest liar of all time." The travel book attributed to Mandeville, which first appeared around 1371, was certainly one of the most popular books of the late Middle Ages (hundreds of medieval manuscript copies of it have survived to the present day), and it was definitely filled with bizarre fabrications. But Browne's assessment of Mandeville's character is undermined by the fact that Mandeville probably never existed.

The Travels of Sir John Mandeville described the travels of an English knight who left England around 1322 and journeyed throughout Egypt, Ethiopia, India, Persia, and Turkey. The stories that Mandeville returned with were fantastic, by any measure. He told of islands whose inhabitants had the bodies of humans but the heads of dogs, of a tribe whose only source of nourishment was the smell of apples, of a people the size of pygmies whose mouths were so small that they had to suck all their food through reeds, and of a race of one-eyed giants who ate only raw fish and raw meat. All of this fantasy was interwoven with other geographical descriptions that were perfectly accurate.

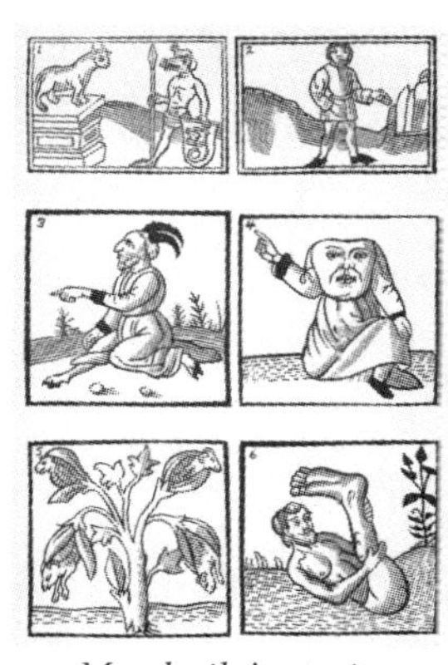

Mandevile's stories

The authorship of Mandeville's Travels remains unknown. Historians cannot decide whether the author was French or

English, though they agree that the book was originally composed in French. The character of Mandeville, as already indicated, was almost certainly fictitious. The name might have been adapted from an earlier French romance titled Mandevie that also involved a hero who embarked on an imaginary journey.

It is not clear how seriously medieval readers took Mandeville's stories. It is tempting to think that they must have recognized them as works of fiction, but it can be a mistake to project too much modern skepticism onto the medieval world. Medieval culture made sense of the world by viewing it through the lens of religious imagery and fantastic legends. So in this respect the book did offer a truth, of a kind, though not one that modern readers are likely to grasp.

18 The Beale Cryptograms

It was 1885 and James B. Ward of Lynchburg, Virginia, was ready to give up. After twenty years of puzzling over a difficult problem with limited success, Ward knew that he had little or no chance of solving the whole thing. He decided to throw the problem open to the public and see if anyone else could be successful. For this reason, he published a pamphlet with the lengthy title: The Beale Papers containing Authentic Statements regarding the TREASURE BURIED in 1819 and 1821, near Bufords, in Bedford County, Virginia, and Which Has Never Been Recovered.

In this pamphlet Ward told a strange story. Ward wrote that according to letters written from Thomas J. Beale to Robert Morriss, Beale had led a party of thirty men west in 1817 on a buffalo hunt in northern New Mexico. While out west they discovered a rich vein of gold and gave up hunting in favour of mining. By 1819 they had accumulated a large store of gold. According to the account

...the question of transferring our wealth to some secure place was frequently discussed. It was not considered advisable to retain so large an amount in so wild and dangerous a locality, where its very possession might endanger our lives; and to conceal it there would avail nothing, as we might at any time be forced to reveal its place of concealment.

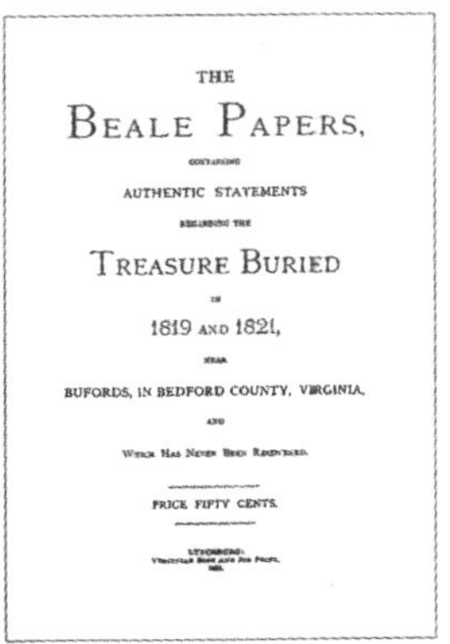
THE

BEALE PAPERS,

AUTHENTIC STATEMENTS

TREASURE BURIED

1819 AND 1821,

BUFORDS, IN BEDFORD COUNTY, VIRGINIA,

PRICE FIFTY CENTS.

Cover page of Beale Papers

The men decided to move their horde by wagon back to Virginia. They brought it back in two shipments and buried the gold in iron pots in a secret vault roughly lined with stone some six feet beneath the ground. The treasure consisted of 2,921 pounds of gold and 5,100 pounds of silver, as well as jewels obtained in St. Louis to save transportation. In 1982 one journalist investigating the Beale story estimated the modern value of the treasure to be 30 million dollars.

According to Ward's writings, the group entrusted their secret to Robert Morriss of Lynchburg while they traveled back to west to get a third shipment. Morriss was given a strongbox with instructions not to open it for ten years. If the men failed to return by then, Morriss was to open the box. Inside the box were instructions and a series of cryptograms. Morriss would have been given keys he would need to decode them. He was to use the secret information in the cryptograms to uncover the treasure and disperse the money among the men's surviving relatives.

Morriss was true to his word. When the men did not return he not only waited ten years, but twenty-three. When he opened the box he found three cyptograms and a letter of explanation. The cryptograms consisted of a series of numbers from one to three digits long. Morriss, who was never given the promised keys to the messages, worked to decrypt them for years, but failed. About a year before his death in 1863 he passed the box onto Ward. Ward, by accident, solved one of the cryptogram ciphers. He was able to decode the message by consecutively numbering the words in the Declaration of Independence, then swapping those words with the matching numbers in the cipher number 2. The message he was able to decode gave him a list of the vault's contents. The other two messages, which were supposed to carry the location of the treasure and the list of men who were part of the group, Ward failed to decrypt after many years of trying.

Ward blamed his financial problems on his compulsive pursuit of an answer to the two remaining cryptograms. To put the matter behind him he decided to make the whole affair public: .... I resolved to sever at once, and forever, all connection with the affair, and retrieve, if possible, my errors. To do this, and as the best means of placing temptation beyond my reach, I determined to make public the whole matter, and shift from my shoulders my responsibility to Mr. Morriss.

After Ward published his pamphlet many people tried to decode the messages. Most failed. A few decided that they succeeded, but their decryptions were faulty, leading to wrong conclusions. Many spent small fortunes themselves digging up Virginia hillsides trying to find the treasure. In 1966 a Tennessee banker employed a backhoe to dig up a considerable chunk of land with no result. A bulldozer was used to level most of a hill on Purgatory Mountain without any better luck.

Between 1897 and 1912, two brothers, George and Clayton Hart, took up the Beale challenge. They spent much of their spare time looking for documents that might serve as keys for the other two ciphers much as the Declaration of Independence had been for cipher 2. Though they never managed to decrypt the messages, that didn't stop them from digging at what they considered promising sites. To this end they even employed a psychic, but still found nothing.

In 1968 the Beale Cypher Association was founded. This group hoped that by pooling their resources and talents they might finally solve the mystery, but though they have been successful in documenting the story of the Beale papers, they have not found the treasure.

Will this mystery ever be solved? Some have suggested that the solution lies not with treasure, but with trickery. What if the Beale papers are a hoax?

One of the first clues that the Beale papers are not what they seem is in one of the documents which is a letter from Morriss to Ward. He states – It was in the month of January, 1820, while keeping the Washington Hotel, that I first became aquainted with Beale...

A notice in the Lynchburg Virginian for December 2nd, 1823 shows that Morriss didn't become the proprietor until three years later. In addition, the Washington Inn wasn't known as the Washington Hotel until after Morriss sold it.

Some of the wording in the Beale papers doesn't seem to fit with the time either. For example, a letter from Beale dated 1822 talks about "stampeding" a herd of buffalo. The word stampede (from the Spanish estampida) did not enter into print before 1844, twenty-two years after the letters supposed date.

In fact there is no solid evidence that a Thomas Jefferson Beale existed in Virginia in the early 19th century. Also there are no records of an expedition that found gold in California. The original Beale papers themselves do not even exist. Ward reported they had been lost in a fire at Virginia Job Print plant along with many of the pamphlets.

If the Beale letters are a hoax there are probably three candidates for the hoaxster. Beale himself, Morriss and Ward. Clearly most skeptics focus on Ward. He published the pamphlet and charged for each copy. Statistical studies of the word usage in the pamphlet suggest that probably all the texts in it were written by a single person, most likely Ward.

Little is known about Ward, but unlike Beale, he clearly did exist. Ward grew up in the same section of Virginia as figures in the Beale papers story. It is believed he was a member of the Freemasons. Records show he joined Dove Lodge No. 51 in 1862. In fact, Ward's membership in the organization may give clues to motives he may have had for concocting a hoax.

Many of the elements in the Beale Papers' story show up in Masonic rites. The idea of a vault (the exact word used by Beale) filled with treasures and lined with rough stone is part of Masonic symbolism. Joe Nickell, a skeptic researching the Beale tale concluded in his book Mysterious Realms:

...Beale and his treasure are illusory – merely part of an allegory meant to evoke the anticipated Masonic `discovery of the secret vault and the inestimable treasures.The contrast between the futile quest for gold and that for more spiritual wealth are didactically expressed in the allegory...

Where did Ward get the inspiration for his story? Several people have pointed to Edgar Allan Poe's story *The Gold Bug* which had similar elements in it. Also, a Kentucky legend about a man named Swift who discovered a silver mine may have influenced Ward. If the Beale Papers are only a story, what about the two undecyphered messages? Are they merely random series of numbers? In 1971 Dr. Carl Hammer did a computer study of the undecyphered messages and concluded that there were cyclic patterns in the numbers that suggested they were not just random, but most likely text-encoded in the same manner as the decoded cipher number two.

So what would the undeciphered messages tell us? The location of a priceless treasure? Or a confirmation that the story is a fabrication by Ward? Until somebody can decipher the messages, if that is possible, we will never know.

OO

Michelangelo's Cupid - Stupid

In 1496, when he was a young man, Michelangelo sculpted a sleeping cupid. He, or an accomplice, then buried it in acidic earth to give it an appearance of great age. The plan was to pass it off as an antiquity, which would allow it to fetch a higher price.

Michelangelo'

The artificially aged sculpture was sold through a dealer to Cardinal Raffaello Riario of San Giorgio. Eventually the Cardinal learned of the forgery, and he demanded his money back from the dealer. However, the Cardinal was so impressed by Michelangelo's obvious talent that he didn't press charges against the young artist. To the contrary, he allowed him to keep his percentage of the sale.

Michelangelo's cupid eventually came into the possession of the d'Este collection in Mantua, where it was reportedly displayed side by side with a genuine antique sleeping cupid. But it is believed that the statue was destroyed in a fire in 1698. Even though it was a "fake", it would be considered priceless today, if it still survived.

OO

Martin Guerre - ???

Martin Guerre, a French peasant, married Bertrande de Rols in 1538. She bore him one son. But in 1548, after a falling out with his father, Martin disappeared. Eight years passed without any sight of him. Because of Catholic law, Bertrande could not remarry. But in 1556 Martin suddenly returned. Or did he?

The man who claimed to be Martin Guerre was similar in appearance and knew many details of Guerre's life. Bertrande accepted him as her husband, and lived with him for three years, bearing him two children. But when the new Martin sued his uncle for part of the inheritance of his father, the uncle became suspicious and accused him of being an impostor. Specifically, the uncle claimed that the new Martin was actually Arnaud du Tilh, a man from a nearby town.

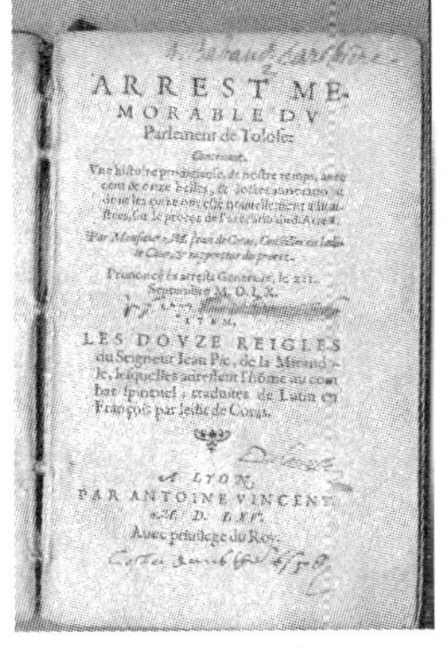
ARREST MEMORABLE DV
Parlement de Tolose

LES DOVZE REIGLES

A LYON,
PAR ANTOINE VINCENT.
Auec priuilege du Roy.

Title page of Arrest Memorable, a contemporary account of the case of w:Martin Guerre

The case went through a series of trials and appeals. The court seemed to be favouring the authenticity of the new Martin, until suddenly the original Martin Guerre showed up. He had been serving in the Spanish army, where he had lost a leg.

The fake Martin Guerre was executed. The real one eventually reconciled with his wife, who bore him another child.

A film based on the story of Martin Guerre was released in 1982.

OO

21 UFO Lands in London

On March 31, 1989 thousands of motorists driving on the highway outside London looked up in the air to see a glowing flying saucer descending on their city. Many of them pulled to the side of the road to watch the bizarre craft float through the air. The saucer finally landed in a field on the outskirts of London where local residents immediately called the police to warn them of an alien invasion. Soon the police arrived on the scene, and one brave officer approached the craft with his truncheon extended before him. When a door in the craft popped open, and a small, silver-suited figure emerged, the policeman ran in the opposite direction. The saucer turned out to be a hot-air balloon that had been specially built to look like a UFO by Richard Branson, the 36-year-old chairman of Virgin Records. The stunt combined his passion for ballooning with his love of pranks. His plan was to land the craft in London's Hyde Park on April 1. Unfortunately, the wind blew him off course, and he was forced to land a day early in the wrong location.

Richard Branson's UFO

OO

Robinson Crusoe or The Native of Formosa

Those who travelled on European roads at the start of the eighteenth century must have met many unusual characters, but one character they might have met would have proven more unusual than the rest. He was a young man who claimed to be from the faraway land of Formosa (now known as Taiwan).

There were just a few problems with the young man's claim of Formosan nationality. First, his skin was white, and his hair was blond. Second, he spoke fluent Latin (which wouldn't be a problem in and of itself), but he did so with a hint of a Dutch accent.

Still, at the beginning of the eighteenth century most of the world remained a mystery to Europeans, and so they had no idea what a real Formosan should look like. They only knew that Formosa was a very distant land where the people undoubtedly had very different customs. And this man certainly had different customs. He occasionally babbled in an unknown language. He worshipped the sun and the moon. He slept upright in a chair with a lamp burning, and he ate heavily spiced raw meat. What better evidence of foreignness could anyone possibly want?

In 1702 the man from Formosa (he had no other name at that time) arrived in Holland and met a Scottish clergyman called William Innes who was serving in the English army. Innes probably saw through the deception right away, but he also knew a good thing when he saw it. He knew that it would help his career if he could present the church with an exotic convert.

So Innes converted the Formosan to Anglicanism, baptised him with the Christian name George Psalmanazar, and brought him to England to meet the Bishop of London. The Bishop embraced

George Psalmanazar

him with open arms, as did the rest of British high society. The elite ladies and gentlemen of England treated Psalmanazar as an exotic curiosity. Even the Royal Society took an interest in him.

Psalmanazar was able to convince many Protestants of the truth of his story by appealing to their religious prejudices, particularly their anti-Jesuit prejudice. He claimed he had been fooled into leaving Formosa by a disguised Jesuit missionary. This story played to the widespread paranoid belief that the Jesuits were sending secret agents throughout the world to trick foreign nations into converting to Catholicism. Protestants figured that if this young man didn't like Jesuits, then he must be worthy of their trust.

But of course, Psalmanazar's story did not convince everyone, especially not the Jesuits. The Jesuit Father Fontaney, who was travelling through England at that time, challenged Psalmanazar to a debate which Psalmanazar accepted. But the debate proved inconclusive because Fontaney didn't know enough about Formosa to seriously challenge any of Psalmanazar's claims. For instance, when Fontaney asked Psalmanazar why his skin was not darker in colour like that of other people from Asia, Psalmanazar replied that in Formosa the members of the nobility lived indoors and therefore had lighter skin than the labourers who worked outside. For all anyone in England knew, this could very well have been true.

Psalmanazar capitalized on his fame by publishing a book titled *An Historical and Geographical Description of Formosa*, in which he offered British readers an intriguing and sensational glimpse at Formosan culture. He claimed that in Formosa convicted murderers were hung upside down and shot full of arrows, that polygamy was allowed, and that every year 20,000 young boys were sacrificed to appease the gods (this latter claim was accompanied by a gruesome illustration of 'The Gridiron upon which the hearts of the young Children are burnt'). Psalmanazar also obtained an appointment at Oxford College to translate religious literature into Formosan.

But despite the apparent success of Psalmanazar's scheme, doubts continued to circulate about his true identity. These doubts became harder and harder to ignore until finally, in 1706, Psalmanazar confessed to his imposture, supposedly motivated by a religious experience that convinced him of the sinfulness of his deception. He spent the rest of his life working as an editor and a writer on Grub Street. At one point he even contributed a section about Formosa to a work titled *Geography of the World*, though this article, unlike his previous book, was truthful. Many years later, he wrote a long confession titled Memoirs of ****, commonly known by the name of George Psalmanazar. This work was published posthumously in 1765, a year after his death.

Who was Psalmanazar really, and why did he perpetrate this deception? Surprisingly little is known about his true identity. In his memoir he claimed to be of French Catholic heritage. He wrote that he adopted the life of a vagabond after growing bored with his studies as a young man. While on the road he discovered that posing as a foreigner was a convenient way to con funds from sympathetic strangers. But he claimed that the deception only rose to a greater level because of the ambition of the clergyman Innes. Given Psalmanazar's record of dishonesty, it is not clear whether this explanation is the truth, or yet another of his fabrications.

23 The Charlton Brimstone Butterfly

Shortly before his death in 1702, butterfly collector William Charlton (1642-1702) sent a specimen to esteemed London entomologist James Petiver. Petiver thought it was quite remarkable. He wrote, "It exactly resembles our English Brimstone Butterfly (R. Rhamni), were it not for those black spots and apparent blue moons on the lower wings. This is the only one I have seen."

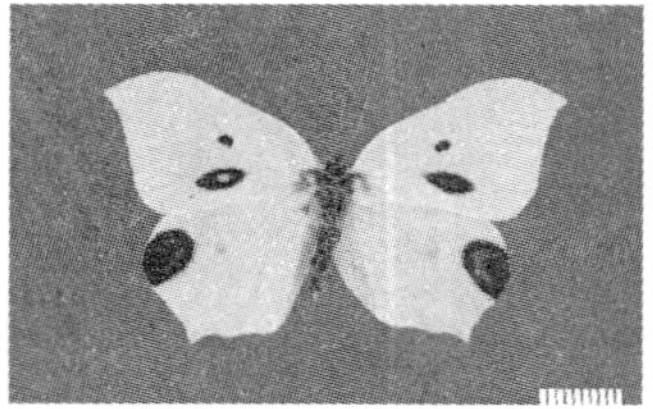

The Charlton Brimstones butterfly

Carl Linnaeus had a chance to examine the rare butterfly in 1763 and declared it to be a new species that he named Papilio ecclipsis. He included it in the 12th edition (1767) of his Systema Naturae.

But thirty years later, in 1793, the Danish entomologist John Christian Fabricius examined it more closely and realized it was a fake. The black spots had been painted on the wings. The rare butterfly, the only one of its kind ever seen, was nothing more than a common Brimstone (Gonepteryx rhamni).

When Dr. E.W. Gray, keeper of National Curiosities at the British Museum where the specimen was stored, heard of the deception, he is said to have become so enraged that he "indignantly stamped the specimen to pieces". The lepidopterist William Jones carefully created two replica specimens that are now preserved as "The Charlton Brimstones".

It is unclear whether this is an example of scientific fraud (i.e. Was Charlton hoping he would be credited with the discovery of a new species?), or if it was intended as a mere practical joke.

OO

The Newark Decalogue: Fact or Fiction?

In November of 1860, amateur archaeologist David Wyrick made an interesting discovery. His excavation exposed a small rock, perhaps seven inches long, composed of "black limestone." The stone had been carved so that one side showed a robed, bearded man. Around the man and then along the sides and back of the object were carved what turned out to be a condensed version of The Ten Commandments. The commandments were written in ancient Hebrew with a peculiar form of post-Exilic square lettering. The artifact itself had been contained in a small stone box that had obviously been hollowed out precisely to contain the carved stone. Nearby, a small stone bowl, about the size of a teacup, was also found.

The carved stone, which was to become known as the Decalogue, seemed to be designed to fit into the hand, and even showed wear marks where it had come into contact with the owner's fingers and a nub where it might have been tethered to the left arm. Researchers concluded that it was a Jewish arm phylactery or tefilla from the Second Temple Period (20BC-70AD). Such an object would have been used by its owner in his daily prayers.

This object would have been an interesting, but not controversial, find if located in the Mideast. The problem was that Wyrick had been excavating an ancient Indian mound near Newark, Ohio, USA.

Why was this Hebrew artifact found in the American Midwest? Most scholars suspected the Decalogue was a hoax: A fake artifact planted where it should not have been either as a joke or to prove some outrageous archaeological theory. In fact, many books list

The finding at Newark

the case of the Decalogue as that of a "well-known hoax" though there is little evidence to back up such a statement.

Wyrick himself became the primary suspect to many of those who thought it was a hoax. A few months before finding the Decalogue, Wyrick had also discovered another strange stone in a different section of Newark. It was shaped like a fat, rounded arrowhead and became known as the Keystone. It too was inscribed with Hebrew lettering with one phrase on each side:

Holy of Holies
King of the Earth
The Law of God
The Word of God

The finding of two strange artifacts by the same person seemed to fuel suspicions of Wyrick as a hoaxer to later archaeologists. However, in 1861 Wyrick had published some of his discoveries in a pamphlet. The picture Wyrick drew of the Decalogue had some 38 different errors in the lettering as well as mistakes in the reproduction of the Moses figure (for example the Decalogue shows Moses wearing a turban, while Wyrick drew him with a beret). It seems unlikely that Wyrick, if he were attempting a hoax, would have made these kind of errors in drawing an object he had carved himself.

Similarly, Wyrick also made mistakes drawing the keystone by having the inscription TWRT YHWH appear as HWRH YHWH.

In 1991 archaeologist Stephen Williams in his book *Fantastic Archaeology* suggested that Wyrick may have planted these stones because he was interested in proving the Lost Tribes of Israel wound up in Ohio. There seems to be little evidence for this as a motive since Wyrick never mentions this theory in the pamphlet he wrote or in his letters. Wyrick's interests, published in the Ohio Farmer in 1860, include mound exploration, surveying, geo-magnetism, anomalous boulders, river terraces, beaver dams and sorghum processing, but not the lost tribes of Israel. It also seems unlikely that if Wyrick had gone to all the trouble of faking the Decalogue he would have figured out he needed to use a pre-Exilic style of lettering (which was in use at the time the lost tribes disappeared) instead of the more modern square post-Exilic style.

The Rev. John W. McCarty, a local minister, and Elijah Sutton were also accused of planting the stones by archaeologist Bradley T. Lepper. Lepper's evidence against the two seems very thin. Bradley based his argument on the speed of which McCarty was able to translate the stone despite its strange lettering. Sutton was a stonecutter who lived in the area (he carved Wyrick's tombstone). He became a suspect because the Decalogue was about the same thickness as that of the monuments he often worked on.

In defense of the two, J. Huston McCulloch, of Ohio State University, points out that any well-trained minister of the time could probably have done the translation in a few hours once he had figured out how to substitute the unfamiliar letters in the text with familiar ones. According to McCulloch, McCarty also published a second article a few days after the first one correcting errors he'd made in the translation. One of the errors, his mistaking the figure on the stone for Christ instead of Moses, was rather obvious in retrospect and it seems unlikely the Reverend would purposefully make it.

The case against Sutton as McCarty's accomplice is even weaker. While the Decalogue is the same thickness as a tombstone, they are composed of different types of rock.

Perhaps the best candidate for a hoaxer, if there was one, was John H. Nicol. In 1864 two additional Hebrew-inscribed stones were found during the excavation of a mound east of Newark. They became known as the Inscribed Head and the Cooper Stone. Shortly after they were found, Nicol, a local dentist, admitted that he had carved them and introduced them into the excavation with the intention of showing how easily the Decalogue and Keystone could have been faked. The Inscribed Head reads in Hebrew letters as:

J-H-NCL

Short vowels in Hebrew are not represented by letters so this is how one would write:

J-H-NiCoL

The Nicol hoax helped discredit the Decalogue and Keystone at the time and some even suspect that Nicol was responsible for carving the original stones. The character of the carving in the Decalogue seems totally different than that of the Nicol stones, though, and Nicol never attempted to take credit for making them.

In 1867 another stone was found near the mound where the Decalogue was discovered. This coffin-shaped stone is now lost, but records show that it was about three inches long and covered with text which seems similar to that on the Decalogue. The fact that the stone was discovered independently from Wyrick (who had died in 1863) seems to confirm that the original find might be genuine.

So are the Decalogue and Keystone hoax or history? If they are genuine, what were Hebrews of the Second Temple Period doing in the American Midwest? If they are fakes, who carved them and why?

Recently attention has been focused on one final piece of evidence. Remember the small stone bowl found near the Decalogue? Who would take the trouble to carve a stone bowl? Among other people, the ancient Hebrews of the Second Temple Period. Under Jewish law stone vessels were always ceremonially pure. Mideastern

Archaeologists use the presence of stone vessels as one of the markers that tells them an ancient site was occupied by Jews.

Los Lunas Decalogue

Ancient copies of The Ten Commandments do not just show up in the New World carved on small stones in Ohio. The Los Lunas Decalogue is cut into a 90-ton basalt boulder on the side of Hidden Mountain, New Mexico. It is inscribed in Hebrew using the Old Hebrew alphabet and some Greek letters. The inscription was first seen by an archaeologist in 1933 and there are reports of it extending back into the 1880's. The writing is on a forty-degree angle, indicating the boulder has shifted since the carving was made. One geologist estimates the age of the work (based on the weathering) could be between 500 and 2000 years old.

Analysis of the text suggests the writer's primary language was Greek, with Hebrew as a secondary language. One scholar suggests that the Decalogue is a Samaritan mezuzah. Similar to the Jewish mezuzah placed by the entrance of a house, a Samaritan mezuzah was traditionally carved on a large stone slab placed by the gateway to a property or synagogue.

25 The Fossils of Dr. Beringer

Dr. Johann Bartholomew Adam Beringer (1667-1740) was a Senior Professor and Dean of the Faculty of Medicine at the University of Würzburg in Germany. Like many physicians of the time, he cultivated an interest in natural history. In particular, he was intrigued by what was called the study of oryctics, or "things dug from the earth." Today we would call this the study of fossils, or paleontology.

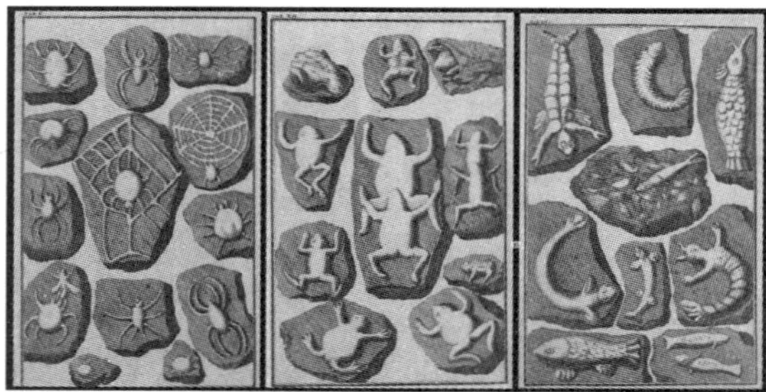

The Fossils of Dr. Beringer

Beringer kept a collection of interesting fossils he had acquired over the years. Until 1725 his collection was quite ordinary, but then, on May 31, 1725, some remarkable new pieces came into his possession. They were delivered to him by three local boys he had paid to explore nearby Mount Eivelstadt and bring him any interesting objects they might find.

What the boys brought him were three stones that displayed, on their surfaces, images in sharp, three-dimensional relief. One stone bore a stylized image of the sun. The other two bore images of worms.

Dr. Beringer was genuinely puzzled by the stones, and he grew even more puzzled as, over the course of the subsequent months, the boys continued to bring him more of these curiosities. By November they had brought him almost two thousand stones bearing the images of plants, insects, birds, snails, astronomical objects, and even Hebrew letters.

Beringer decided he should write a treatise about the stones, in order to bring them to the attention of other scholars. He published this treatise, titled Lithographiae Wirceburgensis, in early 1726.

Beringer devoted the bulk of his book to presenting different theories about what the stones might be. He considered whether they were relics of the Great Flood, or whether they were the product of "the marvelous force of petrifying moisture." He even wondered whether they were the work of man. For instance, could the stones "be ascribed to the superstitious art of the heathen Germans"? Or were the stones of more recent origin? In Chapter XII, Beringer considered whether the stones might be a modern fraud. Ultimately Beringer rejected the idea that the stones were man-made. He felt that there were simply too many of the stones for a modern hoaxer to have produced them all. Nor could he imagine why anyone would want to expend so much energy to pull off such an elaborate hoax. He concluded that the stones had to be the work of nature, though he didn't know what natural process had created them. He left that question to his fellow scholars to debate.

According to legend, just as the first copies of his book were rolling off the printing press, the boys presented Beringer with a final stone, one which had his own name carved in it. Finally, he realized that he had indeed been the victim of an elaborate hoax. Humiliated, and in a state of panic, Beringer frantically tried to buy up all the existing copies of his book. Extant copies of the book are now extremely rare and can fetch over $10,000.

As Chapter XII of the Lithographiae Wirceburgensis demonstrates, Beringer was well aware of the possibility of a hoax before he decided to go to press. He wrote in that chapter:

With peaceful mind and tranquil pen I pursued the dissertation which I had begun on this controversy. Then, when I had all but completed my work, I caught the rumour circulating throughout the city, especially among prominent and learned men, that every one of these stones, which, on the advice of wise men, I proposed to expound in a published treatise, were "recently sculpted by hand, made to look as though at different periods they had been resurrected from a very old burial, and sold to me as to one indifferent to fraud and caught up in the blind greed of curiosity; further, that I, once deceived, in my wretched turn, was deluding the world, and trying to sell new hoaxes as genuine antiques, to the silent laughter of prudent souls." I was shocked beyond words to learn that the authors of this atrocious calumny were two men, perhaps best described as a pair of antagonists, whose names I have reason to protect at present – men with whom I was closely associated in numerous functions, former colleagues in the Academic Society.

Despite the possibility of a hoax, Beringer pressed ahead. Evidently he had poured so much effort into the study of the stones that he couldn't bear the thought that all his work had been in vain. Instead, he convinced himself that, despite the rumour, the stones were real. He suggested that his two colleagues might be spreading a false rumour of a hoax in order to undermine his work.

But evidently, shortly after the publication of the book, something did happen to convince Beringer that all the stones were fake. Perhaps it was, as the legend suggests, the occasion of being presented with a stone bearing his own name. Melvin Jahn and Daniel Woolf have suggested that the local Bishop of the Church might have made the situation clear to Beringer.

Once convinced of the hoax, Beringer decided to bring criminal charges against the two men he suspected of the deceit. These two men were J. Ignatz Roderick, Professor of Geography, Algebra, and Analysis at the University of Wurzburg, and Georg von Eckhart, Privy Councillor and Librarian to the Court and the University.

The case came to court on April 13, 1726, and Beringer won a conviction against the men. The transcript of this case, discovered in the Würzburg State Archives in 1935 by Dr. Heinrich Kirchner, is the main source of information we have about the hoax.

Unfortunately, the transcript does not shed much light on the motivation of the hoaxers. We simply learn that they hated Beringer because "he was so arrogant and despised them all."

In the short run, Beringer emerged from the incident in better shape than his hoaxers. Despite later rumours that he was so mortified by the hoax that he died soon thereafter, he actually lived on for fourteen more years and wrote two more books.

By contrast, von Eckhart died four years after the trial. Roderick was forced to leave Würzburg, with a cloud of dishonour permanently hanging over him.

However, history was not kind to Dr. Beringer. The story of the Doctor and the "Lying Stones" ("Lügensteine" as German authors called them) soon spread, and the Doctor's name became a byword for credulity. The popular version of the story that circulated during the subsequent two centuries falsely alleged that Beringer had fallen for a simple student prank, rather than for an elaborate scheme concocted by jealous colleagues. In academic circles, Beringer's story served as a cautionary tale about the danger of wantonly pursuing unsupported hypotheses.

A second edition of the *Lithographiae Wirceburgensis* was published in 1767, twenty-seven years after Beringer's death. It is not clear why the book was republished at this time. In 1963 Melvin Jahn and Daniel Woolf published an English translation of Beringer's book.

OO

BANG 26

Mary Toft and the Bunny Babies

England during the reign of King George I (1660-1727) was full of oddities, shams, and charlatans. King George himself was a bit of an oddity, never bothering to learn English and keeping his wife imprisoned for 32 years. But for sheer strangeness, nothing surpassed the infamous case of Mary Toft of Godalming and her rabbit babies.

Mary Toft and the Bunny Babies

In September, 1726 Mary Toft began to give birth to rabbits. The local surgeon, John Howard, responded to her family's summons and hurried to Mary's house where, to his amazement, he helped her deliver nine of the animals. They were all born dead, and they were actually rabbit parts rather than whole rabbits. Nevertheless, this didn't lessen the amazing fact that she was giving birth to them.

John Howard excitedly wrote to other men of science around the country, urging them to help him investigate this bizarre phenomenon. Soon two prominent men, sent by the King himself, arrived to investigate: Nathanael St. Andre, surgeon-anatomist to the King, and Samuel Molyneux, secretary to the Prince of Wales. Mary explained to these men that she had recently miscarried, but that during the pregnancy she had intensely craved rabbit meat.

After unsuccessfully attempting to chase down several rabbits, she had dreamt that there were rabbits in her lap. The next thing she knew, she was giving birth to rabbits.

In the presence of the doctors, Mary continued to give birth to even more rabbits. The men performed tests to verify the reality of the phenomenon. For instance, they placed a piece of the lung of one of the rabbits in water and noted that it floated. This meant that the rabbit must have breathed air before its death, which could not have happened inside a womb. Amazingly, the doctors ignored this evidence and decided that there was no deception involved – that Mary really was giving birth to the rabbits.

On November 29th Mary was brought to London. By now her case had become a national sensation, and huge crowds surrounded the house where she was kept. But when kept under constant supervision, Mary stopped giving birth to rabbits, and her case quickly began to unravel.

Witnesses came forward who claimed that they had supplied Mary's husband with rabbits. Then, when a famous London physician, Sir Richard Manningham, threatened that he might have to surgically examine Mary's uterus in the name of science, she wisely decided to confess.

She explained that she had simply inserted the dead rabbits inside her womb when no one was looking, motivated by a desire for fame and the hope of receiving a pension from the King. She was briefly imprisoned for fraud, but was released without trial. It is said that she managed to give birth to a normal, human child less than a year later.

John Howard and Nathanael St. Andre, the two surgeons who had most passionately believed and defended her, fared less well. Their medical careers were both ruined.

OO

Planetary Alignment Decreases Gravity

In 1976 the British astronomer Patrick Moore announced on BBC Radio 2 that at 9:47 AM a once-in-a-lifetime astronomical event was going to occur that listeners could experience in their very own homes. The planet Pluto would pass behind Jupiter,

Patrick Moore

temporarily causing a gravitational alignment that would counteract and lessen the Earth's own gravity. Moore told his listeners that if they jumped in the air at the exact moment that this planetary alignment occurred, they would experience a strange floating sensation. When 9:47 AM arrived, BBC2 began to receive hundreds of phone calls from listeners claiming to have felt the sensation. One woman even reported that she and her eleven friends had risen from their chairs and floated around the room.

OO

Madagascar, or Robert Drury's Journal

A book titled *Madagascar*; or Robert Drury's Journal, during fifteen years captivity on that Island was published in England in 1729. In it, Robert Drury described how, almost forty years earlier, he had been shipwrecked off the coast of Madagascar, survived the slaughter of his shipmates by hostile islanders, and then spent the next fifteen years living as a slave, fighting in local wars, taking a wife, and eventually escaping on a slave ship back to England.

The story was accepted as true during the eighteenth century. In fact, it served as one of Europe's main sources of information about the faraway island of Madagascar. But during the nineteenth century scholars started to question almost everything about it. In particular, there were suspicions that the book was actually a fictional account written by Daniel Defoe, author of *Robinsin Crusoe*, and that Robert Drury didn't even exist.

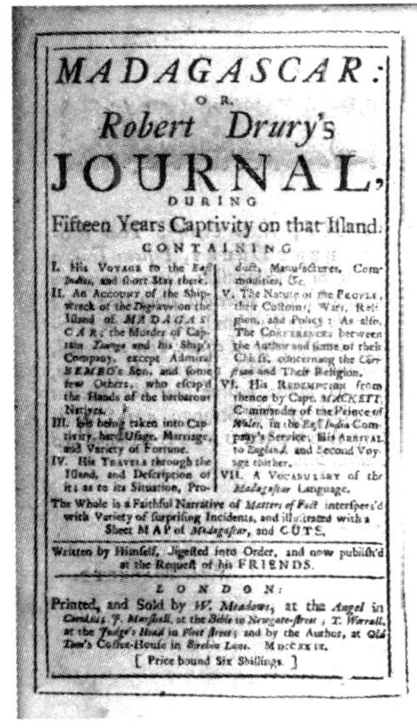

MADAGASCAR:
OR,
Robert Drury's
JOURNAL,
DURING
Fifteen Years Captivity on that Iſland.
CONTAINING

I. His Voyage to the *East-Indies*, and ſhort Stay there.
II. An Account of the Ship-wreck of the *Degrave* on the Iſland of MADAGASCAR; the Murder of Captain *Younge* and his Ship's Company, except Admiral DEMBO's Son, and ſome few Others, who eſcap'd the Hands of the barbarous Natives.
III. His being taken into Captivity, hard Uſage, Marriage, and Variety of Fortune.
IV. His Travels through the Iſland, and Deſcription of it; as to its Situation, Product, Manufactures, Commodities, &c.
V. The Nature of the People, their Cuſtoms, Wars, Religion, and Policy: As alſo, The Conferences between the Author and ſome of their Chiefs, concerning the Chriſtian and Their Religion.
VI. His Redemption from thence by Capt. MACKETT, Commander of the Prince of Wales, in the *East India* Company's Service; His Arrival to *England*, and Second Voyage thither.
VII. A Vocabulary of the *Madagaſcar* Language.

The Whole is a Faithful Narrative of *Matters of Fact* interſpers'd with Variety of ſurpriſing Incidents, and illuſtrated with a Sheet MAP of *Madagaſcar*, and CUTS.

Written by Himſelf, digeſted into Order, and now publiſh'd at the Requeſt of his FRIENDS.

LONDON:
Printed, and Sold by *W. Meadows*, at the *Angel* in *Cornhill*; *J. Marſhall*, at the *Bible* in *Newgate-ſtreet*; *T. Worrall*, at the *Judge's Head* in *Fleet ſtreet*; and by the Author, at *Old Tom's* Coffee-Houſe in *Birchin Lane*. MDCCXXIX.
[Price bound Six Shillings.]

Robert Drury's Journal

However, the controversy has come full circle, because modern scholars suspect the work may not be a hoax after all. In 1996, Mike Parker Pearson, an archaeologist at Sheffield

Mike Parker Pearson

University, published evidence suggesting not only that Drury had lived, but that his description of early 18th century Madagascar was highly accurate... far too accurate to have been invented by Defoe.

Therefore, while it's impossible to say for sure, Robert Drury's Journal may be a case of a factual narrative mistaken for a hoax.

OO

29 The Electric Kite Hoax

On October 19, 1752, the *Pennsylvania Gazette* published a brief description of an experiment recently conducted by Benjamin Franklin. Franklin, the article said, had flown a kite in a thunderstorm, causing electricity to be conducted down the line of the kite and electrifying a key tied to it. This demonstrated that lightning, as many had speculated, was a form of electricity.

Franklin's electric kite

Franklin's electric kite became the most famous experiment of the eighteenth century, helping to make Franklin famous throughout Europe and America. And yet, some historians argue that it probably never happened.

They point to a curious lack of details about the experiment. It is not known exactly when the experiment occurred. Sometime in June, 1752 was the closest Franklin ever came to an exact date. Nor did Franklin ever write a formal report about it. The only witness to the event was Franklin's son, who never said a word about it. Finally, such an experiment would have been extremely dangerous, possibly fatal, as Franklin knew.

Historian Tom Tucker suggests that Franklin originally proposed the idea for the experiment as a joke. Frustrated because the British

Benjamin Franklin

Royal Society had been ignoring his letters to them about his earlier electrical research, he might have proposed the deadly experiment as a subtle joke. It was his way of saying, Go fly a kite in a storm! But when his suggestion reached France, where people took it seriously, Franklin decided to play along and claimed he really had conducted the experiment.

Tucker's theory remains controversial. Other historians argue that Franklin would never have risked being exposed as a liar by the scientific community.

OO

30 The Hitler Diaries

*I*n the autumn of 1979 an investigative reporter for the German magazine Der Stern, Gerd Heidemann, was invited to the house of a man named Fritz Stiefel, a collecter of Nazi memorabilia. Stiefel had paintings and letters created by Hitler laid out in a glass case like a museum display. Heidemann, a Nazi enthusiast, studied each of them carefully. Finally he noticed something else in the case: A black book. When he asked about it he was told that it was a secret diary kept by the Nazi leader. One of supposedly six volumes.

Heidemann was shocked. He'd been fascinated by the life of Hitler for years but never heard that the man had kept a diary. The inner thinking of the Nazi leader had always been a mystery even to other leading members of the Third Reich. A true diary would give historians insight into the thinking of a man who had, for evil, changed the face of the world. Heidemann realized that if the diaries were authentic and if he could get a hold of them, he would have one of the biggest journalistic scoops of the 20th century. To buy the diaries Heidemann knew he would have to have the economic backing of his magazine Stern, but before they would give him the money he would have to make a case for the diaries being authentic.

The Hitler Diaries

One of Heidemenn's first steps was to try and determine how the Stiefel's volume of the diary had gotten into his hands. Stiefel had been told the diary had been aboard a plane carrying some of the Fuehrer's belongings that had crashed in the village of Boernersdorf at the end of the war. The first thing that Heidemann did was to travel to Boernersdorf to confirm the story. There he found that indeed there had been a plane crash in April of 1945. Records indicated that a Junkers 352 transport went down carrying some of Hitler's personal effects. When he heard of the crash Hitler had stated, "In that plane were all my private archives that I had intended as a testament to posterity. It is a catastrophe!"

Heidemann also found that a chest of papers had supposedly been recovered from the wreck and this was rumoured to be the source of the diaries. He also learned there were 27 more volumes of the diaries in the hands of a man named Konrad Fischer.

Equipped with this information, Heidemann made a proposal to his bosses at Stern that they purchase the diaries. Stern said it would pay as much as 2 million marks (approximately $800,000) to obtain the diaries. With this money behind him, Heidemann went searching for Fischer. Fischer turned out to be hard to find. Eventually Heidemann contacted him through intermediaries. Fischer seemed reluctant to sell the diaries, but the amount of money involved won him over. He did inist that Heidemann promise to keep his identity a secret.

The first diary was delivered to Stern editorial offices in January of 1981. Surprisingly more and more diaries kept showing up. Heidemann told his bosses that after the plane crash the diaries had come into the possession of an East German general and were being smuggled out of that country one by one (supposedly inside pianos). With each new volume Stern paid more money and stood to make more money when they resold the story to other news media. The final tally was 62 volumes (covering the period from 1932 to 1945) for which Stern paid 9.9 million marks (almost $4 million).

Before Stern could resell the story they needed to make sure the diaries were authentic. To do this they had handwriting experts compare the diaries with copies of material found by Heidemann in the German Federal Archives at Koblenz. Without question the handwriting was identical and Stern's editors enthusiasm for the project soared, perhaps blinding them to the need for additional authentication checks.

On April 25th, 1983, Stern magazine broke the story. The cover, showing one of the black bound volumes, proclaimed "Hitlers Tagebucher Entdeckt" or "Hitler's Diary Discovered." The news media around the world jumped on the story. Newsweek, ParisMatch and London's Sunday Times and Times newspapers all made bids to get the rights to reprint all or part of the diaries. Stern stood to make a fortune on the reprint rights.

What the diaries showed was surprising. If one were to believe the diaries, Hitler was a much more kinder and gentler man than the historical record showed. In particular, the diary entries suggested that he had little knowledge of what was happening in the concentration camps scattered around Europe. He also expressed a desire to deport the Jews to other countries rather than put them to death.

Even before skeptics got a look at the material they expressed doubts that the diaries were real. Historians familiar with Hitler pointed out that he loathed to write and that none of his intimates in the Nazi organization, including his secretary, had believed he had kept a diary. When the critics actually got to look at the material their objections to its authenticity only increased. Historian David Irving pointed out that what was recorded in the diaries did not correspond to known historical events and the materials that the books were composed of appeared to be too modern for the era. Most damaging of all was the claim by experts of Hitler's writing that the script in the diaries did not resemble his at all, especially since the handwriting had been at the heart of Stern's authentication procedure.

West Germany's Federal Archives decided to get involved and ran several scientific tests on the books. On May 6, 1983, they released their findings: the paper, ink and glue of the diaries was undoubtedly manufactured after the end of World War II and Hitler's death. The volumes for which Stern had paid millions of dollars were worthless forgeries.

Stern realized that it had been taken and heads began to roll. Several members of the staff (including Heidemann) were fired. In addition Stern's founder, Henri Nannen, filed fraud charges against Heidemann several days later and the police began to investigate. It quickly became clear that Heidemann had not forged the diaries himself. Heidemann gave up Fischer's name and the investigation soon focused on him. The police soon discovered that Fischer's real name was Konrad Kujau. Kujau was a petty criminal who specialized in forgery. He had started by taking legitimate Nazi memorabilia and adding the names of important Nazis to increase the value. Later on he started forging entire works including letters, documents and even paintings and sketches allegedly done by Hitler. In a 1983 book by Billy Price called Adolf Hitler: The Unknown Artist a quarter of the works pictured were actually forgeries by Kujau.

Kujau's prolific forgery solved the mystery of how the Stern handwriting experts had been fooled. When they had compared the handwriting in the diaries to the handwriting found in letters by Hitler, they pronounced it identical. Indeed it was. The letters that they had used for comparison turned out to be previous forgeries by Kujau, not actually letters written by Hitler.

Kujau, Heidemann and Kujau's wife, Edith, were brought to trial. Kujau claimed that Heidemann was completely aware that the documents were forgeries but bought them anyway paying 1 million marks. Heidemann claimed he hadn't known they were forgeries but admitted that he had seen the possibility of some historical discrepancies. Kujau and Heidemann were given four and one half years in prison and Edith eight months. The judge stated that while there were only three defendants, the Stern's publishing firm should be the fourth. He said that Stern had "acted with such naiveté and negligence that it was virtually an accomplice in the fraud."

Nobody ever found out what happened to the bulk of the money paid out by Stern. According to Kujau, Heidemann skimmed much of it before paying him. Clearly both Kajau and Heidemann's lifestyle took a turn for the better at the time of the fraud and most of the money never made it back into Stern's hands.

Could Stern really have avoided the loss of millions of dollars and its international reputation? It seems clear in retrospect that the publishing firm could have found out the truth if they had simply subjected the diaries to a few scientific tests. Examination of the books themselves showed that they contained whiteners and threads not manufactured until the 1950's. Chemical tests revealed that the ink was modern and only recently applied to the paper.

A careful reading of the text would have also revealed historical inaccuracies that might not have proved the diaries fake by themselves, but should have raised suspicions. Much of the material Kujau stole from a book called *Hitler's Speeches and Proclamations* written by Max Domarus. This also should have raised a red flag to anyone carefully trying to authenticate the diaries.

As the judge indicated, the owners and editors of Der Stern may have been as much to blame as Kujau and Heidemann. They were too ready to believe that they had scooped every news organization in the world on the the story of the Hitler diaries, and much too ready to profit from it.

31 The Turk

Enlightenment thinkers were fascinated by machines called automata whose sole purpose was to mimic living objects, and they built some amazing examples of them. The Frenchman Jacques de Vaucanson built a mechanical duck that quacked, ate food, and defecated just like the real thing. But no automaton was more praised or more famous than the Great Chess Automaton of Baron Wolfgang von Kempelen.

The Great Chess Automaton consisted of a wooden figure dressed in Turkish clothes (and usually referred to as the 'Turk') whose trunk emerged out of a large wooden box filled with gears and wires. When wound up, the figure played chess against human opponents.

The Great Chess Automaton

But this wasn't a machine that simply mimicked the movements of a man playing chess. The Great Chess Automaton actually moved pieces on its own, planned strategy, and responded to the actions of its opponent. To top it all off, it was an excellent player. It almost always won. In other words, this was not a mere mechanical contraption, such as Vaucanson's duck. This, in the words of its inventor, was an actual 'thinking machine.'

Kempelen, who was a Hungarian nobleman, built the chess automaton in 1769 and toured throughout Europe with it, exhibiting it before audiences filled with royalty and aristocrats. He typically invited audience members to challenge his automaton to a match, and these challengers invariably lost. The automaton even defeated Benjamin Franklin.

In 1790 Kempelen finally dismantled the machine and stored it away. But this was not the end of its career, because in 1805, after Kempelen had died, his family sold the machine to Johann Nepomuk Maelzel, a German university student.

Maelzel reconstructed the automaton and toured with it throughout Europe before bringing it to America in 1826. There it again entertained and fascinated audiences, while regularly beating challengers.

The means by which the automaton operated was a source of constant speculation. Before each show, Kempelen made a point of opening sliding doors on the side of the box to prove that it was occupied only by clockwork gears, and each time the automaton moved the noise of grinding machinery could be heard. Still, most people suspected that there had to be someone hidden in there, somehow. They just couldn't figure out how. Perhaps, they theorized, it was a dwarf. But there were also many who were convinced that the automaton was an actual thinking machine.

While it was touring America, Edgar Allan Poe had a chance to watch it in action, and he wrote an article in which he tried to use strict logic to solve its mystery. He theorized that a man was hidden in the body of the turk itself. He was almost right, but not quite.

The real secret was revealed on February 6, 1837, almost seventy years after the automaton's creation, in a tell-all article published by the Philadelphia National Gazette Literary Register. Hidden inside the box out of which the body of the Turk emerged (not in the body of the Turk, as Poe thought) was a full-sized man. The identity of the hidden man varied, but Kempelen and Maelzel tried to use chess champions, one of whom wrote the exposé. Among the chess masters who served as the automaton's hidden operator were Johann Allgaier and Aaron Alexandre.

A series of sliding panels and a rolling chair allowed the automaton's operator to hide while the interior of the machine was being displayed. The operator then controlled the Turk by means of a 'pantograph' device that synchronized his arm movements with those of the wooden Turk. Magnetic chess pieces allowed him to know what pieces were being moved on the board above his head.

So the Great Chess Automaton was not sentient after all, but only a hoax. This disclosure proved its undoing. Its mystery snatched away, it was relegated to a warehouse, where a few years later, in 1854, it perished in a fire.

32 William Henry Ireland's Shakespeare Forgeries

As literacy rates rose during the eighteenth century, a kind of cult-like reverence for the work of William Shakespeare emerged. Theaters staged his plays repeatedly, and collectors eagerly sought out any relics related to his life.

The bookseller Samuel Ireland was one of the most passionate of these Shakespeare-worshiping relic hunters. He devoted his life to the pursuit of Shakespeariana, in the process neglecting his talented young son, William Henry Ireland (1777-1835). That is, until his son brought home from the law office where he worked a mortgage document apparently signed by Shakespeare himself.

William Henry Ireland

At the time William Henry brought home the Shakespeare document, in 1794, he was only eighteen. He claimed he had found the document among the estate papers of a client who desired to remain anonymous. Samuel Ireland was ecstatic at what his son had found, and grew even more so when William continued to bring home other spectacular finds, including a love letter written by Shakespeare to Anne Hathaway and eventually a previously unknown historical drama by the Bard titled Vortigern.

Arrangements were made for Vortigern to be performed at the Drury Lane Theatre on April 2, 1796. The theater's owner half-suspected a fraud, but decided that there was enough public interest in the play, whether or not it was a fake, to warrant a performance.

The actors, however, were more skeptical and not so willing to play along. To indicate their displeasure, they hammed their way through the performance, and when the lead actor, J.P. Kemble, arrived at the line "And when this solemn mockery is ended," he delivered it with such emphasis that everyone in the audience knew he was referring to the play itself. This prompted an outburst of laughter and applause.

After that infamous opening night, the play was never performed again. A few weeks later William Henry confessed that the play and other documents were all his own work. His father, however, refused to believe the confession and insisted until the day he died that the Shakespearean treasures his son had brought home all had been real.

OO

33 Hotheaded Naked Ice Borers

*I*n its April 1995 issue *Discover* Magazine announced that the highly respected wildlife biologist Dr. Aprile Pazzo had discovered a new species in Antarctica: the hotheaded naked ice borer. These fascinating creatures had bony plates on their heads that, fed by numerous blood vessels, could become burning hot,

Hotheaded Naked Ice Borers

allowing the animals to bore through ice at high speeds. They used this ability to hunt penguins, melting the ice beneath the penguins and causing them to sink downwards into the resulting slush where the hotheads consumed them. After much research, Dr. Pazzo theorized that the hotheads might have been responsible for the mysterious disappearance of noted Antarctic explorer Philippe Poisson in 1837. "To the ice borers, he would have looked like a penguin," the article quoted her as saying. *Discover* received more mail in response to this article than they had received for any other article in their history.

OO

Billy Tipton or ??

Billy Tipton (1914-1989) got his start in the predominantly masculine world of jazz during the 1930s. He made a name for himself playing the saxophone and piano, and during the 1950s formed his own group, the Billy Tipton Trio. Throughout his life he had a number of wives and adopted three sons. Therefore, when he died at the age of 74 on January 21, 1989, it came as a surprise to almost everyone to discover that Billy Tipton was really a woman. Even his wives claimed not to have known his secret during their marriages to him.

Billy Tipton

Billy Tipton (middle) trio

It is not clear why Tipton chose to conceal his gender. Some speculate that it was the only way for Tipton to make it in the world of jazz during the 1930s, although by the 1950s a number of women had established careers in that field. Others theorize that Tipton was simply more comfortable living as a man.

Regardless of Tipton's motivation, it was certainly a secret that he rigorously guarded. Apparently he chose not to seek medical treatment for the bleeding ulcer that killed him because that would have required disclosing his gender to the hospital staff.

Ironically, by the 1980s the revelation that a male musician was actually a cross-dressing woman would no longer have been shocking to most people, given that this was the decade in which musicians such as Madonna, Boy George, Prince, David Bowie, and Dawn Lang all made careers out of bending gender norms.

35 Grimm's Fairy Tall Tales

The Grimm's Fairy Tales, first published in German in 1812 as Kinder- und Hausmärchen, is considered to be one of the major works of 19th-century culture. Popular myth holds that the tales came from simple, peasant folk interviewed by the brothers, Jakob and Wilhelm. In reality, the bulk of the tales came from a handful of middle- and upper-class women. Some of the tales were French in origin, not German. Furthermore, the tales were heavily revised and rewritten by the Grimm brothers before publication.

Jacob and Wilhelm Grimm (an 1843 drawing)

In his 1983 book *One Fairy Story Too Many: The Brothers Grimm and their Tales* John Ellis argued that the Grimm Brothers engaged in a kind of literary fraud. As Ellis put it, "the Grimms deliberately made false claims for their tales and suppressed the evidence of their actual origin."

Most scholars, however, are more kind to the Grimms. They agree that the tales did not come from peasant folk, but argue that the Grimms did not try to hide or misrepresent their sources. They attribute the Grimm's revision of the tales to their attempt to synthesize different versions of the tales together.

OO

36 The Great Moon Landing Hoax

On July 20, 1969, astronaut Neil Armstrong set his boot on the surface of the lunar landscape. In that act he completed one of mankind's greatest achievements: Landing a man on the moon.

Or did he? Some skeptics have suggested that those trips the Apollo spacecraft made to our nearest celestial neighbour may never have happened. According to these skeptics it was all an elaborate deception designed to make the world believe that the United States had beat the USSR to the moon after NASA figured out that they didn't have the technology to do it for real.

Photograph of astronaut Buzz Aldrin, lunar module pilot of the first lunar landing mission, beside the United States flag as taken by astronaut Neil A. Armstrong

Bill Kaysing, author of *We Never Went to the Moon*, is perhaps the most well-known skeptic of the manned moon landings. Kaysing was also a heavy contributor to a television special entitled Conspiracy Theory: Did We Land on the Moon? The program, hosted by Mitch Pileggi, first appeared on the Fox network in 2001 and has been repeated several times since then.

The program raised a number of points that on first glance seem to make NASA's moon landing suspicious. On close scientific examination, however, most of these claims seem to fade like moonshine in the morning sun.

Perhaps the first point raised, or at least the one most memorable, is the stars. Or more precisely, the lack of them. People who are skeptical of the moon landing point out that even though the sky in all the moon pictures is black, as it should be if there is no atmosphere on the moon (and there isn't), no stars can be seen. This is taken as an indication that the pictures were faked and NASA forgot to paint stars on the studio backdrop.

The truth is that if you were to see stars in the sky in those moon pictures it would be a definite indication that they were faked. Why? Well, all the landings were done during daylight hours on the moon. That means that even though the sky was black, the sun was up. The lunar surface is mostly a light gray and reflects light extremely well. The light levels during the landings were probably similar to those in a western desert in the morning, bright enough to warrant sunglasses, or in the case of the astronauts, sunvisors on their spacesuits.

For this reason the NASA cameras had to be stopped down (this mean a minimal amount of light was allowed to enter the camera) and the exposure times shortened to allow only enough light onto the film to properly illuminate the surface. The stars were much too faint to show up on these pictures. Expecting them to show up would be similar to going out into that western desert at midmorning, setting the camera properly to take pictures under those conditions, coming back after nightfall to take pictures of the stars without readjusting the exposure on the camera and then expecting to get something. Stars are hard enough to photograph under any conditions, let alone with an exposure setting appropriate for daylight.

Ironically, many of the conceptual drawings of the moon landing done by NASA artists at the time show stars appearing in the lunar sky. It seems unlikely NASA would have forgotten to paint them on the backdrop if they were trying to fake it.

Even modern NASA pictures of the space shuttle or earth from orbit do not usually show stars. This is for the same reason: When in direct sunlight the earth and shuttle are very bright and the cameras must be stopped down too low to capture starlight. Moonlanding skeptics point out that if the photographs the astronauts supposedly took on the moon were actually taken there, the shadows should be absolutely black. The sun is the only source of light and there is no atmosphere to scatter the light around. In the images, though, the shadows are often well lit. Skeptics use the argument that this was because the shots were filmed in a studio that had an atmosphere.

There is a basic misconception with this thinking, however. In a single light situation, shadows are filled in not just from the light rays being scattered by air. The light in the shadows also comes from being bounced off other objects. You can see this effect from a simple home experiment. Get two pieces of construction paper, one black and one white, then go into a dark room and light a single lamp. Place an object in front of you to create a shadowed area. Now bring the black construction paper near the shadow on a 45-degree angle partly facing the light, partly facing the shadow. Because the black paper is absorbing the light, the shadow does not change. Now slide the white construction paper in front of the black. The shadow should grow lighter from the light reflecting off the white paper.

The same effect is present on the moon. The light bounces off the surface of the moon as well as the astronauts spacesuits and other equipment around the lander. Because the moon's surface is a light gray, and very reflective, the shadows can be lit very brightly.

Another argument often used to disprove the authenticity of the Apollo photographs involves the direction of the shadows. According to skeptics, the shadows in the NASA pictures appear to diverge. If the sun is the single bright light in the pictures, then the shadows should be parallel. This, according to NASA's critics, shows that the single light source was much closer to the astronauts than the sun, or there were multiple lights involved.

Clearly there were no multiple lights involved as there are no multiple shadows in the pictures. Whether the shadows appear to diverge, instead of running parallel is dependent on the camera lens used in taking the photographs. A slightly wide-angle camera, as was used on the moonwalk, can make parallel lines appear to diverge. Even so, some photographs (like the one to the right of Alan Shepard planting the flag) do not show any divergence at all, but the parallel shadows converge on the photo's vanishing point, just like they should.

While the American flag was being put up on the moon it appears to wave. Skeptics argue that this was caused by a breeze on the set where the hoax was filmed because a flag cannot wave in a vacuum. This is wrong thinking, however. The flag waves because the astronauts were wiggling the flagpole back and forth trying to get it to stick in the lunar soil. Given that kind of motion, any cloth would wave whether it is in a vacuum or not.

Later on, still pictures show the flag apparently waving even after the astronauts have moved away from it. A glance at the moving video reveals that the flag is not waving. It simply had a ripple in it from not being fully extended across its length as it hung from its top supporting pole much like a gathered curtain. This was done accidentally on Apollo 11, but the astronauts loved this effect so much that they did it on every subsequent moonlanding.

The van Allen belts are a region in space where Earth's magnetic field has trapped particles from the solar wind. Skeptics of the moon landing argue that an astronaut would get a lethal dose of radiation if he were to pass through the belts on the way to the moon.

While continued exposure to the concentration of radiation found in the belts might well be fatal, the space capsule the astronauts were traveling in was going very fast and passed through the belts in a few hours. The metal hull of the capsule also gave the astronauts some protection from the radiation as well. While there was a certain risk in passing through the belts, as there is in every venture into space, the astronauts exposure from the van Allen belts was minimal: about 2 rem which is the equivalent of a 100 chest x-rays.

There are any number of points skeptics of the moon landing can bring up that don't "look right" to them, but all have simple scientific explanations when examined closely. Let's try doing the opposite: Look at some things seen on the video or in the pictures that would indicate that these things really happened on the moon.

Phil Plait of the Bad Astronomy site points outs that video footage taken of some of the moon rovers shows dust being thrown up by the wheels as it rolls across the lunar surface. The dust rises and falls in nearly a perfect parabolic arc. This can only happen in a vacuum. Dust thrown up in earth's atmosphere would float and swirl around as it was carried by eddies in the air. Wherever the rover was at the time the video was taken, it was certainly in a location that had no air. Skeptics might argue that NASA took the trouble to build a sealed set and pump the air out, but this would be a tremendously difficult undertaking. It would also contradict evidence of the "waving" flag, as described above.

Astronaut Dave Scott also did a quick physics lesson in front of the video camera during Apollo 15 that showed he was on the moon. He dropped a hammer and a feather and watched them fall to the ground. On Earth the feather's high wind resistance and low weight would have caused it to drift down slowly. On the moon, however, the feather fell just as quickly as the hammer. Both dropped to the ground at exactly the same rate one would expect to see if the objects were being pulled to the ground by the moon's one-sixth Earth gravity.

Even without the above evidence, the claim that the Apollo mission to the moon was fabricated by NASA makes little sense. For a conspiracy of silence to be effective, those involved must be very few in number. Every additional person added to the conspiracy raises the chances that somebody will, accidentally or on purpose, "spill the beans."

In the case of the Apollo program hundreds of thousands of people were involved. Not only NASA employees, but also the companies who were contractors of NASA for the project. Even if you argue that most of the contractors and much of NASA staff did not have to be in on the hoax, we are left with thousands of people who had direct knowledge of the events. Starting with the NASA employees that saw the astronauts climb into the rocket to the hundreds of sailors on the recovery ship that saw them emerge out of the space capsule when the trip was over.

There are also hundreds of scientists that analyzed the rocks returned from the moon and had no doubt that they were authentic. The moon rocks brought back by the Apollo missions are not like anything else on Earth. They show the effect of billions of years exposure to vacuum, no moisture, and high energy cosmic rays. They are also pitted with tiny meteoroids. None show the burned effect typical of meteorites that have landed here on Earth. Could they have been faked? No. As one geologist put it, "It would be easier to just go to the Moon and get one."

The producers of Conspiracy Theory: Did We Land on the Moon? are undoubtably intelligent people who had the opportunity to research their subject thoroughly before filming their documentary, yet they seemed to have completely missed many of the simple explanations for the questions they raise. It makes one wonder: Who are the real hoaxers in this story?

OO

Charles Waterton's Nondescript

Charles Waterton was a famous English eccentric and naturalist. In 1821, he returned to England from an expedition to Guiana, bringing with him hundreds of specimens of South American wildlife, carefully stuffed and preserved. His boat docked in Liverpool, and a customs inspectors named Mr. Lushington boarded. Lushington took one look at the exotic specimens that Waterton had piled up in crates and ordered that a hefty fee should be paid for their importation. Waterton protested. After all, the specimens were of greater scientific value than they were of commercial value. Nevertheless, Lushington would not bend. He insisted that Waterton pay the highest import tax possible.

Three years later Waterton travelled again to Guiana. Upon his return to England he bore with him this time the head of a fabulous specimen which he described as the 'Nondescript.' It looked very much like the head of a person, though the exposed face was surrounded by a thick coat of fur. Waterton claimed he had encountered and killed this man-like creature in the jungles of Guiana.

Waterton later wrote a book about his travels through Guiana, titled Wanderings in South America. In this book he included a dramatic description of how he had hunted down the Nondescript. Accompanying this description was an illustration of its head.

Generations of readers enjoyed Waterton's colourful book, but no one has ever again encountered a Nondescript in the wild. The actual taxidermically preserved specimen that Waterton brought home with him provides the strongest argument in favour of its

Charles Waterton and his Nondescript (right)

existence. But naturalists who have examined the specimen have suggested that the face is molded out of the hind quarters of a howler monkey.

Adding a touch of humour to this mystery, is the rumour that the Nondescript bears a startling resemblance to Mr. Lushington, the overzealous customs inspector who had caused him so much grief back in 1821. The suspicion is that Waterton, in his own peculiar way, was literally trying to 'make a monkey' out of the tax collector.

BANG

38 The Fortsas Bibliohoax

Jean Nepomucene Auguste Pichauld, Comte de Fortsas, was a man with a singular passion. He collected books of which only one copy was known to exist. If he ever discovered that one of the volumes in his library had a duplicate anywhere in the world, he would immediately dispose of it. So when he died on September 1, 1839 he possessed only fifty-two books, but each of them was absolutely unique.

His heir, not sharing the old man's passion for book collecting, arranged for an auction to sell off the library, and so a catalogue of this small but highly unusual collection was mailed to bibliophiles throughout Europe. The auction, the collectors were told, was to be held in the offices of Mâitre Mourlon, notary, 9 rue de l'Église, in Binche, Belgium on August 10, 1840.

When Europe's librarians and intellectuals received the catalogue, they could scarcely believe their eyes. The books would have been valuable even if duplicate copies had existed, but the fact that each one was unique made them priceless. The catalogue contained detailed descriptions of the books, as well as numerous comments. A typical comment read:

A manuscript note attributes this work to Pere Felix Grebard, private secretary to the noted Huet, bishop of Avranches. This Pere Grebard is likewise the author of a very rare tragedy, 'La mort de Henry le grand,' which I have had in my collection, but of which I rid myself, having learned that Mons. J. Ketele of Audenarde had another copy of it.

On August 9, the day before the auction, the collectors descended on Binche like a pack of vultures. The Belgian government even sent an official representative, believing that the collection was so valuable that it should be bought in its entirety and kept in the country.

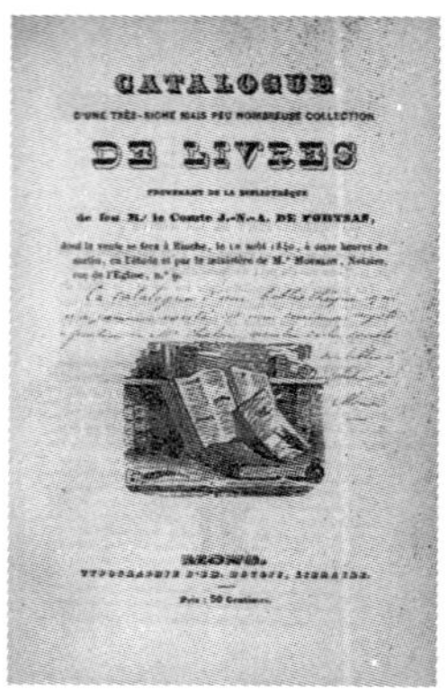

The catalogue

But only disappointment greeted the hopeful buyers. Try as they might, they could not locate any street named "rue de l'Église" in the town of Binche.

Their spirits sunk even lower when they read an announcement in the newspaper informing them that the town of Binche had decided to purchase the entire collection for its public library.

Disheartened, some of the collectors returned home, but others stayed, curious to view the unique books in their new home. But although they searched and searched, they couldn't find the library anywhere. Only then did it gradually dawn on them. There was no Binche public library. There was no Comte de Fortsas. The entire auction and list of unique books had been an enormous, elaborately designed hoax.

The man behind the hoax was a local antiquarian named Renier Hubert Ghislain Chalon (1802-1889). The planning that had gone into the deception was incredible. He had carefully researched the interests of all the major bibliophiles in Europe in order to ensure that they would make the long and fruitless trek to Binche. And he had done all this merely for the sake of a practical joke.

The hoax proved not to be a total loss for its victims. The catalogue they had received itself became a highly coveted collector's item. Within a few decades it had more than quadrupled in price.

There was such demand for the catalogue, that the printer of the original catalogue, M. Hoyois, decided to publish a few more copies of it. However, Chalon forbade him from doing so, leading to a legal battle between the two men. This dispute is described in *The Bibliographer: A Journal of Book-Lore* (June, 1884):

In 1855, M. Hoyois issued a prospectus for a reimpression of the Fortsas Catalogue, with the orders and correspondence of various bibliophiles with regard to the supposed sale, and a facsimile of a letter from the Count de Fortsas. M. Chalons forbade this re-impression, and a division arose between the friends. M. Chalons took legal measures to prevent M. Hoyois from reprinting the catalogue, and also influenced the Societe des Bibliophiles Belges to refuse their subscription to the book.

An account of the Fortsas Bibliohoax, from Daniel Tredwell's 1882 A monograph on Privately illustrated Books. A Plea for Bibliomania (pages 81-82), is excerpted below:

The most noted hoax ever perpetrated upon the body elite in literature, was that of Comte de Fortsas' sale catalogue in 1840. The following account of this inimitable affair is an extract from Philes' Philobiblion, volume II., page 75:

In the year 1840, the book collectors in Europe were greatly excited by the publication of the sale catalogue of the Count J.N.A. de Fortsas. This little volume of only fourteen pages contained a list of the books which formed the Count's collection, composed of only fifty-two articles, each of them unique. The Count would keep no book in his collection, if he found it mentioned by any bibliographer. No wonder the bibliographical world was excited.

The sale was to take place in the office of a notary of Binche, an insignificant village of Belgium. The catalogues were sent to the great collectors of France and England, and each recipient supposed himself specially favoured, and each kept his own secret. It is said that Brunet, Nodier, Techener, Renouard and other bibliophiles of Paris met in the stage to Binche, each one having hoped to steal away unnoticed and have the game all to himself.

M. Castian, of Lisle, who was greatly interested in the treasures of this sale (particularly in a work published by Castman, of Tournay, relating to the Belgian revolution of 1830, the entire edition of which had been suppressed, this copy fortuitously being saved), seemed a little incredulous about this wonderful collection, and took the precaution to make some inquiries as he was passing through Tournay concerning the book, and called on the publisher. M. Castman had forgotten it, but his foreman recollected it, and the author, M. Ch. Lecocq, perfectly. This at once silenced his suspicions.

The Baron de Reiffenberg, then the Director of the Royal Library of Brussels, asked for an appropriation to purchase some of these treasures, which was granted. His commission to purchase covered the entire catalogue, save seven articles which were thought to be too free for a public library. One enthusiastic bookseller made the journey to Binche from Amsterdam, only to see one volume, the Corpus Juris Civilis, printed by the Elzevirs on vellum. The Princess de Ligne, anxious to destroy the record of her ancestor's achievements, and to protect the reputation of the grandmothers of the best families in the state, wrote to M. Voisin to buy No. 48 at any price: "Achetez, je vous en conjure, a tout prix, les Sottises de Notre Polisson de Grandpere."

The Roxburghe Club was represented; and, singularly enough, every book from the catalogue appealed with peculiar force to the taste or weakness of some distinguished collector, and each one was the fortunate possessor of a catalogue through the post.

Tradition says that the good people of Binche, seeing their town invaded by a rusty and serious-looking set of strangers, all inquiring for the office of the same notary who had no existence, began to suspect some plot against the liberties of the state, and consulted about the propriety of putting as many of them as their limited accommodations would permit under confinement.

On the morning of the sale the newspapers contained a notice that the bibliographical world would learn with regret that the library of Count de Fortsas would not be sold, the town of Binche having resolved to keep it together in honour of the Collector, their townsman.

The force of the hoax could go no further. For the whole affair was a hoax. The Count de Fortsas was a myth – his chateau, his passion, his success in bibliographical pursuits, were apocryphal. And yet M. Chalons, a French collector, admitted to a stageful of bibliophiles, whom he met on the road, to have had the pleasure of a long personal acquaintance with the count.

He is said to have been the author of this witty practical joke.

OO

39 Lamarckian Inheritance

During the 1920s an Austrian scientist named Paul Kammerer designed an experiment to prove that Lamarckian inheritance (the notion that organisms may acquire characteristics and pass them to their offspring) was possible. His experiment involved a species of toad called the Midwife Toad. Most toads mate in water – resulting in scaly black bumps on their hindlimbs which allow them to hold on to each other during mating, but the midwife toad mates on land – and therefore does not have these lumps. Kammerer said that by forcing midwife toads to mate in water, he could prove that they would develop the same bumps.

Paul Kammerer

Kammerer mated a number of generations of toads in a fishtank full of water. Eventually he announced that he had succeeded and he presented a group of midwife toads with black bumps on their hindlimbs.

However, in 1926, Dr G. K. Noble studied the famous toads and discovered that the black bumps were in fact ink that had been injected in to the hind legs of the toads. When the fraud was unveiled in 1926, Kammerer was humiliated. He insisted that he had not injected ink into the toads and suggested that one of his lab assistants might have done it. Kammerer committed suicide a few days later.

The Feejee Mermaid Mystery

*I*n mid-July, 1842, an English gentleman named "Dr. J. Griffin", a member of the British Lyceum of Natural History, arrived in New York City bearing a remarkable curiosity – a real mermaid supposedly caught near the Feejee Islands in the South Pacific. The press were expecting him, since throughout the Summer they had been receiving letters from Southern correspondents describing the doctor and his mermaid. So when he checked in to his hotel, reporters were waiting for him, demanding to see the mermaid. Grudgingly he obliged. What they saw totally convinced them of the creature's authenticity.

Soon after this, the showman P.T. Barnum visited the offices of the major papers where he explained that he had been trying to convince Dr. Griffin to display the mermaid at his museum. Unfortunately, the doctor was unwilling to do so. So Barnum volunteered to give the papers use of a woodcut of a beautiful, bare-breasted mermaid that he had prepared, since it was now useless to him. The papers (each thinking they had an exclusive) happily accepted the offer, and on Sunday, July 17, mermaid woodcuts appeared in all the papers. Simultaneously, Barnum distributed ten thousand copies of a pamphlet about mermaids throughout the city. The mermaids in the pamphlet were also represented as seductive ocean maidens.

With all this publicity, anticipation to see the Feejee Mermaid (as it was now being called) became enormous. (Note: it's also often spelled Fiji or Fejee.) It was the main topic of conversation throughout the city. Everyone was talking about whether it was a real mermaid. They had to see it for themselves. So Dr. Griffin agreed to exhibit it for a week at Concert Hall on Broadway.

Huge crowds showed up for the exhibit. Dr. Griffin lectured for these crowds about his experiences as an explorer and described his theories of natural history. These theories were a bit peculiar. For instance, his main argument was that mermaids must be real since all things on land have their counterpart in the ocean – sea-horses, sea-lions, sea-dogs, etc. So therefore, we should assume there are also sea-humans! Meanwhile, the press continued to lavish attention on the mermaid, with rave reviews appearing in papers, such as this from the New York Sun:

The Feejee Mermaid

"We've seen it! What? Why that Mermaid! The mischief you have! Where? What is it? It's twin sister to the deucedest looking thing imaginable – half fish, half flesh; and 'taken by and large,' the most odd of all oddities earth or sea has ever produced." (The New York Sun, August 5, 1842.)

After the week-long engagement at Concert Hall, Dr. Griffin agreed to allow the mermaid to stay longer in New York City. So it was moved to Barnum's American Museum, where it was exhibited for a month "without extra charge." Ticket receipts at the museum promptly tripled.

Throughout all this, the deception of the public had been three-fold. First, although advertisements had shown the mermaid to have the body of a young, beautiful woman, the creature itself was far less attractive. It had the withered body of a monkey and the dried tail of a fish. As a correspondent from the Charleston Courier put it: "Of one allusion... the sight of the wonder has forever robbed us – we shall never again discourse, even in poesy, of mermaid beauty, nor woo a mermaid even in our dreams – for the Feejee lady is the very incarnation of ugliness." In his autobiography, Barnum later described the mermaid as "an ugly, dried-up, black-looking, and diminutive specimen... its arms thrown up, giving it the appearance of having died in great agony."

Second, Dr. Griffin was a fraud. He was no English gentleman. In fact, there was no such thing as the British Lyceum of Natural History. Griffin's real name was Levi Lyman, and he was Barnum's accomplice-in-deception. The mermaid's introduction and exhibit had been the brainchild of Barnum all along. Barnum had arranged for letters about Dr. Griffin to be sent to New York papers throughout the Summer, and had then carefully orchestrated the mermaid publicity once Dr. Griffin (Lyman) "arrived" in New York. This had all been done to give the mermaid a veneer of scientific respectability.

Finally, the mermaid itself was a fake, and Barnum knew it. He had leased the mermaid from Boston showman Moses Kimball (who, in turn, had bought it from a seaman), but before doing so Barnum had consulted a naturalist to inquire about the mermaid's authenticity. The naturalist had assured him it was quite fake. Nevertheless, Barnum realized that it wasn't important whether or not the mermaid was real. All that was important was that the public be led to believe that it might be real. So he hired a phony naturalist (Dr. Griffin) to vouch for the creature's authenticity, placed pictures of bare-breasted mermaids in the newspapers, and thereby manipulated the public into wanting to see it. As Barnum's biographer A.H. Saxon puts it, the Feejee Mermaid was a classic example of Barnum's ability to "take a mildly interesting object that had been around for some time and to puff it almost overnight into an earthshaking 'event.' "

Barnum himself didn't create the Feejee Mermaid. As noted, he merely leased it from Moses Kimball. In fact, the creature had already enjoyed quite a colourful history before Barnum transformed it into a celebrity.

The Feejee Mermaid was an example of a traditional art form perfected by fishermen in Japan and the East Indies who constructed faux mermaids by stitching the upper bodies of apes onto the bodies of fish. They often created these mermaids for use in religious ceremonies. The Feejee Mermaid herself is believed to have been created around 1810 by a Japanese fisherman. It was bought by Dutch merchants who then, in 1822, resold it to an American sea captain, Samuel Barrett Eades, for $6000 (at the time, a huge amount of money). Eades had to sell his ship in order to afford the mermaid, but he hoped to make a fortune by exhibiting it in London. (Unfortunately for him, he didn't own the entire ship, and this later proved to be a problem for him.)

By September, 1822 Eades had made it back to London with the mermaid, and it did prove to be a popular attraction. But it never made a fortune for him. Eades wasn't as good a showman as Barnum would later be. In addition, British naturalists who had a chance to examine the mermaid soon debunked it in the press, dampening the public's interest in it. Then Eades was sued by the other owner of the ship. The courts ordered Eades to pay back the money he had embezzled by serving the shipowner without pay until he repaid his debt. Eades sailed the seas for the next twenty years, trying to repay the debt. But he never did. When he died, ownership of the mermaid passed to his son, who promptly sold it to Moses Kimball for a fraction of what his father had bought it for.

After Barnum had exhibited the mermaid for a month at his Museum, he decided to send it on a tour of the Southern states. He entrusted his uncle, Alanson Taylor, with this responsibility. Barnum anticipated an uneventful tour, but this was not to be. When Taylor and the mermaid arrived in South Carolina, they found themselves embroiled in a bitter feud between two rival newspapers, the Charleston Courier and the Charleston Mercury, with the mermaid as the focus of the dispute.

The problem began when Richard Yeadon, editor of the Courier, wrote a review of the mermaid in which he declared his belief that she was real. Simultaneously, a local amateur naturalist, the Rev. John Bachman, published a review in the Mercury in which he blasted the mermaid as a crude humbug created by "our Yankee neighbours." This difference of opinion quickly escalated into a bitter argument. (So bitter that, if not for the intervention of "mutual friends," it might have ended in a duel.) This dispute brought an early end to the Southern tour, and the Feejee Mermaid had to be secretly shipped back to New York.

For the next twenty years the Feejee Mermaid split her time between Kimball's museum in Boston and Barnum's museum in New York. Her biggest adventure occurred in 1859, when Barnum took her with him on a tour of London. When Barnum returned from London in June, 1859, he brought her back to Kimball's museum. This would prove to be the last place we know that she was. After this, her whereabouts are unknown.

According to one theory, she was destroyed when Barnum's museum burned down in 1865. But this is unlikely, since she should have been at Kimball's Boston museum at that time. More likely, she perished when Kimball's museum burned down in the early 1880s. Harvard's Peabody Museum of Archaeology and Ethnology does possess a mermaid that some have speculated might be the original Feejee Mermaid. According to their records, this mermaid was saved from the fire that consumed Kimball's museum and was later donated to Harvard by Kimball's heirs. The problem is that the Peabody's mermaid doesn't look anything like what we would expect the Feejee Mermaid to look like. It's much smaller and far less skillfully crafted. So the real Feejee Mermaid probably met her end in the 1880s.

But although the Feejee Mermaid is gone, her memory lives on in popular culture. "Feejee Mermaid" has become the generic term for the many fake mermaids that can be found around the world in sideshows, behind bars, or at the back of curiosity shops. (For San Diego residents, one can be seen up in Leucadia.) The Feejee Mermaid herself also made an appearance in an episode of the X-Files ("Humbug," Season 2, Episode 20).

OO

The Surgeon's Photo's Hoax

In 1993, Christian Spurling, stepson of the flamboyant movie maker and big game hunter "Duke" Wetherell, admitted he'd made the "monster" out of some plastic and a clockwork, tinplate, toy submarine. The picture (Often referred to as the "Surgeon's Photograph," because Colonel Robert Kenneth Wilson, a physician, claimed to had taken it by the Loch in April of 1934) had withstood careful scientific examination. Monster fans had speculated that the pictures showed a plesiosaur, while skeptics said it must have been an otter head or tree trunk. Nobody seems to have suspected it was actually a toy submarine.

According to two Loch Ness researchers, David Martin and Alastair Boyd, in 1993 they'd heard Wetherell's son, Ian, in a 1975 article, had alleged that his father had faked one of the "Nessie" photographs. A couple of things seem to ring true about his statement. First he named Maurice Chambers as a part of the conspiracy. This was the very man Wilson had said he was going to visit the day he took photo. Also Ian Wetherell had mentioned that some of the photos taken that had been included the far shoreline in the image.

Since, with only one exception, every version of the published pictures had the shoreline cropped out, it seemed likely that Ian only knew about it because he'd been there when the photo was taken. Since by then Ian Wetherell was dead, the two men decided to talk to Ian's stepbrother, Christian Spurling. When Martin and Boyd visited him, Spurling, then 93, admitted he'd been approached by Duke Wetherell to build a fake monster.

Duke Wetherell apparently concocted the plan as revenge upon the London Daily Mail newspaper. In 1933 the Daily Mail had hired

Wetherell to find the Loch Ness Monster. Soon after arriving at the lake Wetherell found some strange tracks of a four-toed creature in the soft mud near the water. Wetherell estimated that whatever left the tracks must be twenty feet in length. Plaster casts were taken and sent to the London Museum of Natural History. While the world awaited the Museum's analysis, however, hundreds of monster hunters and tourists showed up at the Loch. Unfortunately after a few weeks the Museum announced that the tracks were not that of an unknown monster, but those of a hippo. Apparently Wetherell himself had been hoaxed. The dried foot used to make the print was probably part of an umbrella stand or ash tray. The Daily Mail was angered at Wetherell and ridiculed and humiliated him.

It was soon after this that Spurling, who was a model-maker by trade, was approached by his stepfather to build the "beast." Construction was done with plastic wood over the conning tower of the toy submarine he'd purchased. The neck, estimated by some from the photograph to be over three feet high, actually measured between 8 and 12 inches.

"We'll give them their monster," Duke told his son. Ian Wetherell and his father took the completed contraption and a camera to the Loch and photographed it on a quiet bay, then sank the evidence

The Surgeon's Photograph is now said to show a fake Nessie made of plastic wood

Nessie hunt goes on after scientists concede hoax

By John Young

A SCIENTIST investigating the existence of the Loch Ness monster refused to dismiss the popular legend yesterday, in spite of the most famous picture of the supposed creature being exposed as a hoax.

Adrian Shine, leader of the Loch Ness and Morar Project, set up to discover whether a mysterious being inhabits the deep waters southwest of Inverness, even welcomed the revelation that the photograph which appeared in the *Daily Mail* in April 1934 was a fraud.

According to new claims, the picture was concocted using a toy submarine fitted with the head and neck of a sea serpent made from plastic wood. It was taken by Colonel Robert Wilson, a Harley Street gynaecologist, who claimed to have seen "something in the water" on April 19, 1934, and has since been known as the Surgeon's Photograph.

Researchers have, however, discovered that Wilson was the front man for a conspiracy to hoodwink Fleet Street led by Marmaduke Wetherell, a self-styled big game hunter, who had been hired by the *Daily Mail* to track down the monster. The other members of the group were Wetherell's son Ian, his stepson Christian Spurling, and Maurice Chambers, an insurance broker, all of whom are now dead.

Hoaxers: Marmaduke Wetherell and Colonel Wilson

Wetherell is said to have been motivated by revenge after his "discovery" of footprints on a beach in Loch Ness was discredited by the Natural History Museum, which said the prints had been made by the dried foot of a hippopotamus, perhaps part of an umbrella stand.

Mr Shine said yesterday that he was convinced that the report of the hoax was valid. Much of the research was carried out by one of his own staff, Alastair Boyd. "It was always a very controversial photograph," he said. When the negative was inspected, the "monster" was found to be very small.

But Mr Shine added, "Eyewitness acounts still suggest that there is something powerful in the loch. As scientists, we naturally resent hoax evidence, because it discredits the seriousness of our research. I hope the whole mystery can now be approached more openly."

in the mud at the edge of the lake. The undeveloped film was then passed to Chambers and on to Colonel Wilson, who had them developed. He then sold them photo to the Daily Mail. The conspirators were quite unprepared for the publicity the photo generated and apparently decided not to admit the hoax. The story stayed unknown for over sixty years.

Not everyone thinks that the photo is a fake. Some have questioned why Martin and Boyd waited to announce the story until Spurling was dead, making it impossible for others to question him. As far as the beast itself goes, not even Boyd thinks that the end of the Surgeon's photo is the end of the Loch Ness Monster. Boyd, who has seen the creature himself, remains a believer.

OO

The Giant Hoax in History

The Cardiff Giant, a gigantic ten-foot tall stone man, emerged out of the ground and into American life on October 16, 1869, when he was discovered by some workers digging a well behind the barn of William C. "Stub" Newell in Cardiff, New York. Word of his presence quickly spread, and soon thousands of people were making the journey out to Stub Newell's farm to see the colossus. Even when Newell began charging fifty cents a head to have a look at it, people still kept coming.

Speculation ran rampant over what the giant might be. The central debate was between those who thought it was a petrified man and those who believed it to be an ancient statue. The 'petrifactionists' theorized that it was one of the giants mentioned in the Bible, Genesis 6:4, where it says, "There were giants in the earth in those days." Those who promoted the statue theory followed the lead of Dr. John F. Boynton, who speculated that a Jesuit missionary had carved it sometime during the seventeenth century to impress the local Indians.

The truth was somewhat more prosaic. It was actually the creation of an enterprising New York tobacconist named George Hull. The idea of burying a stone giant in the ground occurred to him after he got into an argument with a methodist Reverend about whether the Bible should be taken literally. Hull, an atheist, didn't think it should. But the Reverend disagreed. The Reverend insisted that even the passage where it says 'there were giants in the earth in those days' should be read as a literal fact. According to Hull, after this discussion he immediately "thought of making a stone, and passing it off as a petrified man." He figured he could not only use the fake giant to poke fun at Biblical literalists, but also make some money.

Hull's idea turned out to be a stroke of genius. The entire venture cost him over $2,600 (all done with the collusion of the farmer Newell and the stonecutters who carved the giant), but the gamble paid off when a group of businessmen paid $37,500 to buy the giant and move it to Syracuse, where it could be more prominently exhibited.

In Syracuse the giant came under closer scrutiny. Othniel C. Marsh, a paleontologist from Yale, paid it a visit and declared it to be a clumsy fake. He pointed out that chisel marks were still plainly visible on it. These should have worn away if the giant had been in the ground for any appreciable length of time. Sensing that the game was up (and having already cashed out), Hull confessed. But the public didn't seem to care that it was fake. They kept coming to see it anyway. They even began referring to it affectionately as 'Old Hoaxey.'

Recognizing the giant's popularity, the great showman P.T. Barnum offered the new owners $60,000 for a three-month lease of it. When his offer was refused, he paid an artist to build an exact plaster replica of it, which he then put on display in his museum in New York City. Soon the replica was drawing larger crowds than the original. This competition prompted the owners of the giant to file a lawsuit against Barnum, but the judge refused to hear their case unless the 'genuineness' of the original could be proven. Sheepishly they dropped their charges. What is believed to be Barnum's replica of the giant is currently on display in Marvin's Marvelous Mechanical Museum, located outside of Detroit.

The Cardiff Giant

Many have declared the Cardiff Giant to be the greatest hoax of all time. Whether or not this is the case, its huge size and mysterious presence certainly tapped into some strange element of the post-Civil War American psyche. Although the massive public interest in the giant gradually died down, it remained popular. Even today people still make the journey to visit it at its permanent home in the Farmer's Museum in Cooperstown, New York. OO

43 The Sokal Affair

The Sokal affair was a hoax by Alan Sokal (a physicist) perpetrated on the postmodern cultural studies journal *Social Text* (published by Duke University). In 1996, he submitted a paper of nonsense camouflaged in jargon to see if the journal would "publish an article liberally salted with nonsense if (a) it sounded good and (b) it flattered the editors' ideological preconceptions."

Alan Sokal

The paper, "*Transgressing the Boundaries: Towards a Transformative Hermeneutics of Quantum Gravity*", was published in "*Science Wars*" that year. On the day of publication, Sokal announced (in a different paper,) that the article was a hoax. He said that Social Text was "a pastiche of left-wing cant, fawning references, grandiose quotations, and outright nonsense". Much heated debate followed, especially regarding academic ethics.

Another recent example of this same situation is the 2005 Rooter Paper; this was a paper randomly generated by a computer which was submitted – and consequently approved as legitimate – to a scientific conference.

OO

44 The Great Mammoth Hoax

Woolly mammoths became extinct thousands of years ago. But in October, 1899 a story appeared in McClure's Magazine titled "The Killing of the Mammoth" in which a narrator named H. Tukeman described how he had recently hunted down and killed a mammoth in the Alaskan wilderness.

According to the tale, Tukeman was traveling through Alaska in 1890. At Fort Yukon he met an old Indian named Joe whom he showed some pictures from a scrapbook. One of the pictures happened to be of an elephant. Seeing the picture, Joe became excited and told Tukeman he had once seen a similar creature living in a nearby mountain valley.

Woolly mammoths

Tukeman decided to find the creature. He hired an Indian guide, and together the two men traveled to the location described by Joe. Sure enough, they found the creature still there, bathing in a mountain river: "There he stood in a little clearing, the great beast that only one other living man had seen, tearing up great masses of lichenous moss and feeding as an elephant feeds."

Working on the premise that the creature would be attracted to smoke, the two men built a large bonfire, and, as expected, the mammoth eventually rushed over to inspect the blaze. When the animal was near, the two men shot it repeatedly from their hiding place in the trees until it was dead.

As the mammoth was dying Tukeman admitted feeling some guilt: "A feeling of pity and shame crept over me as I watched the failing strength of this mighty prehistoric monarch whom I had outwitted and despoiled of a thousand years of harmless existence." When the mammoth lay dead, the two men carefully preserved its hide and bones by burying them in the ground. Then they roasted and ate some of the meat, finding it "not unpalatable, but terribly tough."

The two men traveled back to San Francisco, where Tukeman met a naturalist called Mr. Conradi. Mr. Conradi offered him millions of dollars to purchase the remains of the mammoth. Tukeman accepted the offer and journeyed back to the site where he had buried the creature, disinterred it, and transferred its remains into Mr. Conradi's possession. The story ended with Tukeman noting, "the most generally accepted theory heretofore has been that Mr. Conradi found the carcass frozen in an iceberg in the Arctic Ocean. The measurements exactly as taken by me, were handed to the Smithsonian, and accepted without question as his own."

This tale was pure fiction, and was labelled as such in McClure's table of contents. Nevertheless, huge numbers of readers were fooled by the realistic tone of the narrative and wrote both to the magazine and to the Smithsonian expressing outrage that the last mammoth had been shot. So many people wrote in that the magazine had to publish a statement in a subsequent issue explaining that "The Killing of the Mammoth" had simply been a work of fiction. Their statement read:

'The Killing of the Mammoth' by H. Tukeman was printed purely as fiction, with no idea of misleading the public, and was entitled a story in our table of contents. We doubt if any writer of realistic fiction ever had a more general and convincing proof of success."

OO

45 The Prince of Abyssinia

On February 7, 1910 the Prince of Abyssinia and his entourage were received with full ceremonial pomp on the deck of the H.M.S. Dreadnought, the British Navy's most powerful battleship. Although the Commander-in-Chief of the Dreadnought had only received a last-minute warning of the Prince's arrival, he had the sailors standing at attention when the Prince arrived. The Abyssinian party acknowledged the greeting with bows as they shuffled onto the ship, dressed in their long, flowing robes, and for the next forty minutes the Commander gave them a guided tour of the vessel. The Abyssinians paused at each new marvel while murmuring the appreciative phrase "Bunga, Bunga!" in their native tongue. Finally the royal visitors departed as "God Save the King!" played in the background.

The Prince of Abyssinia

The next day the Navy was mortified to learn that the party they had escorted around the warship had not been Abyssinian dignitaries at all. Instead it had been a group of young, upper class pranksters who had blackened their faces, donned elaborate theatrical costumes, and then forged an official telegram in order to gain

The Daily Mirror

A newspaper cutting of the hoax

access to the ship. Their ringleader was a man named Horace de Vere Cole, but the entourage also included a young woman called Virginia Stephen who would later be better known as the writer Virginia Woolf.

By February 12 the British newspapers were full of the story of the stunt. "Bunga Bungle!" the Western Daily Mercury trumpeted. For a few days the Navy was the laughingstock of Britain. Sailors were greeted with cries of "Bunga, Bunga" wherever they went. One newspaper suggested that the Dreadnought change its name to the Abyssinian.

Humiliated and furious, the Navy sent the warship out to sea until the episode blew over. It wanted to bring formal charges against the pranksters, but dropped the idea for fear that it would simply attract more publicity to the case. Finally it settled on a more informal punishment. In the style of British boarding-schools, the participants (though not Virginia Stephen) were each symbolically tapped on their buttocks with a cane. None of the participants went on to perpetrate any more hoaxes except for Cole, who was known throughout his life as an inveterate prankster.

OO

46 The Strange Mystery of the Minnesota Iceman

In 1968 two cryptozoologists, Ivan Sanderson, a science writer, and Dr. Bernard Heuvelmans, a Belgian naturalist, thought they'd made the find of the century.

Heuvelmans had been a house guest of Sanderson when the two of them heard about creature, not quite human and very hairy, that was preserved in a block of ice. The creature had been shown in carnivals and fairs across the mid-western United States. Its exhibitor, Frank Hansen, had claimed that it was a "man left over from the Ice Age" and charged 25 cents for a peek at the thing in its refrigerated, glass coffin.

Sanderson and Heuvelmans drove to Hansen's farm where the thing had been stored for the winter. In a cramped trailer they examined the creature and became convinced that they had found a Neanderthal Man, Bigfoot or something similar.

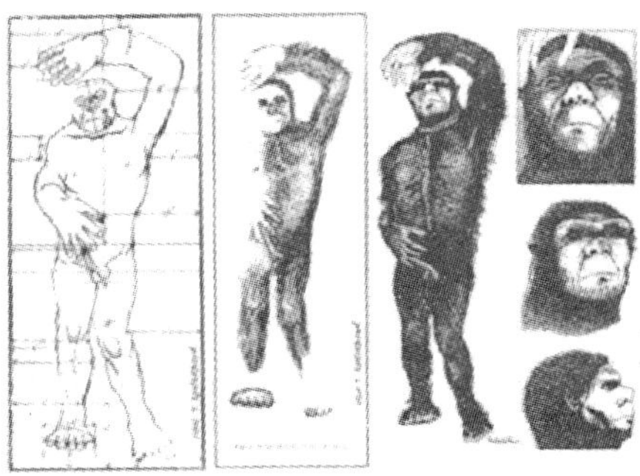

The Minnesota Iceman

After three days of study Heuvelmans believed the beast was authentic. The doctor even smelled the putrefaction where some of the flesh had been exposed from the melted ice. They also discovered that the thing had apparently been shot through the eye. Heuvelmans guessed that the creature had been murdered in Vietnam during the war and smuggled into the United States in a "body bag."

Heuvelmans (on right) with Dr. Boris Porshnev

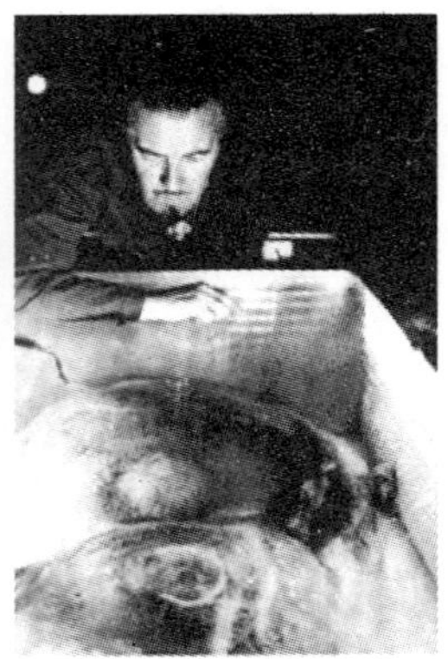

Sanderson examinig the creature

Heuvelmans wrote a paper about the beast for the Institute of Natural Sciences in Belgium entitled, "Preliminary Note on a Specimen Preserved in Ice; Unknown Living Hominid." Sanderson wrote an article, called "Living Fossil," on the same subject for *Argosy* Magazine.

The Smithsonian Institution got involved when Sanderson approached Dr. John Napier about scientifically examining the creature. The Smithsonian, though, found out about the murder theory and asked the FBI to investigate. The head of the agency, then J. Edgar Hoover, declined pointing out there was no law violated if the beast was indeed a non-human. (The incident did give Hansen the opportunity to add a sign labeled "The near-Man ... Investigated by the FBI" when the exhibit went back on the road.)

An additional twist to the murder story occurred when the tabloid, the *National Bulletin*, ran a story in which a woman, named Helen Westring, claimed she'd killed the creature. According to the story Westring had been hunting near Bemidji, Minnesota, in 1966 when the thing had attacked her. She had dispatched it with a shot through the right eye.

At about the same time a Hollywood special effects firm claimed that they had made the "Iceman" in 1967. Howard Ball, who made figures for Disneyland with his son, Kenneth, had modeled the fake in rubber trying to make it look like "an artist's conception of Cro-Magnon man" with "a broken skull with one eye popped out."

Hansen never clearly confirmed or denied that the original creature was a model and, saying that the creature was really owned by a mysterious millionaire, then declined to have it examined further. The Smithsonian lost interest in studying it as they became wary of looking like they had been taken in by a hoax.

Sanderson and Heuvelmans, clearly embarrassed, backed off from their original claims about the creature.

As for the "Iceman" himself, Hansen removed it from exhibition for a while and even reported destroying it, but rumours are it still shows up at carnivals every once in a while.

OO

47 The Piltdown Man

During the early twentieth century the scientific community was eagerly searching for the fossil 'missing link' that would prove an evolutionary relationship between man and apes. In 1907 a jawbone was found in Germany that displayed characteristics of both species. This was the best evidence for a missing link yet, but scientists still wanted something better, something more definitive.

Charles Dawson

Enter Charles Dawson and the Piltdown Man. Charles Dawson was a solicitor who lived in southern England, near Sussex. He was also an enthusiastic amateur paleontologist. In 1908 some workmen, knowing his interest in fossils, presented him with curious bone fragments that they had found while working in a gravel pit near the town of Piltdown. Dawson's interest was piqued and he soon began conducting his own excavation in the pit. Eventually he enlisted the aid of Arthur Smith Woodward, keeper of the Department of Geology at the British Museum.

The real excitement begin in 1912 when Dawson, with Woodward working nearby, found two skull fragments and a very curious jawbone. Given the proximity of the skull fragments and the jawbone to each other, Dawson and Woodward concluded they must have belonged together... that, in fact, they must have been part of the very same skull. This made them extremely excited because, taken as a whole, the skull displayed characteristics of both man and ape. The jaw was ape-like, whereas the upper skull fragments were definitely human. If the jaw and skull fragments did come from the same creature, then they had found the missing link.

In December, 1912 Woodward displayed a reconstruction of the skull at a meeting of the Geological Society of London. Woodward argued that it was the skull of a man, whom he called Piltdown man (after the location where it had been found). He argued that it came from a human who had probably lived about half a million years ago, during the Lower Pleistocene period.

Woodward's claim immediately caused an enormous stir within the scientific community. Many felt that the jawbone and skull were simply too dissimilar to belong together. The jaw, they said, looked far more apish than one would expect to find attached to a high-vaulted, human skull. But Woodward's backers eventually won out and the new species entered the textbooks as Eoanthropus dawson, or "Dawson's Dawn Man."

Over the next few years more fossil objects continued to turn up in the Piltdown pit: animal bones, an object that looked like a cricket bat, and two more skulls. Then, in 1916, Dawson died, leaving Woodward as the main advocate for the Piltdown man.

For over three decades the Piltdown skull was accepted by the scientific community as an authentic artifact. But as more skeletons of early man were found, it became clear that the Piltdown Man was radically unlike anything else in the fossil record. Therefore in 1953 a team of researchers at the British Museum (Kenneth Oakley, Wilfred Le Gros Clark, and Joseph Weiner) subjected the skull and jawbone to a rigorous series of tests. What they found was shocking. The skull was a fake.

Using a fluorine-based test to date the skull, the researchers determined that the upper skull was approximately 50,000 years old. The jawbone, however, was only a few decades old. A second test, using nitrogen analysis, confirmed the first test. They also found that the jaw had been artificially stained with potassium dichromate to make it appear older. The British Museum researchers argued that someone must have taken the jawbone and teeth of a modern ape, probably an orangutan, and stained them in order to make them look ancient. These artifacts, the jaw and skull fragments, must then have been planted at the Piltdown site.

Having proven fraud, the question that remained was who had been responsible for the deception. Woodward had a strong reputation for honesty, and his innocence was generally acknowledged. Dawson, instead, was fingered as the likely culprit. His motive for perpetrating the hoax was complex, since he never profited from it financially. But it seemed likely that he had done it to gain scientific fame and recognition. After the British Museum team published their findings, it was then discovered that Dawson had trafficked in other fake antiquities. This seemed to confirm that he probably was the culprit behind the Piltdown man hoax.

Today most still agree with the verdict that Dawson was the hoaxer, but controversy continues to simmer. Some argue that Dawson worked with an accomplice, perhaps Pierre Teilhard de Chardin, a young priest who briefly participated in the dig. Others place the blame elsewhere entirely. Martin Hinton, an employee at the British Museum whom Woodward once refused a job, has been implicated ever since a boxful of artificially stained bones that may have belonged to him was discovered in 1975. Even Arthur Conan Doyle, author of the *Sherlock Holmes* novels, has been named as a possible suspect. Doyle lived near Piltdown and had a strong interest in paleontology.

Whoever perpetrated the crime, it is considered to be one of the most damaging scientific hoaxes of all time, because it set the development of evolutionary theory back for years while researchers laboured pointlessly to integrate a fake skull into the fossil record.

OO

The War of the Worlds Terrors

On the evening of October 30, 1938, the audience listening to CBS Radio were told they were going to be treated to the music of Ramon Raquello and his orchestra, broadcast live from the Meridian Room at the Park Plaza in New York City. The performance began, but mere minutes into it a reporter from Intercontinental Radio News interrupted to deliver an important announcement. Astronomers had just detected enormous blue flames shooting up from the surface of Mars.

The New York Times.

NEW YORK, MONDAY, OCTOBER 31, 1938.

Radio Listeners in Panic, Taking War Drama as Fact

Many Flee Homes to Escape 'Gas Raid From Mars'—Phone Calls Swamp Police at Broadcast of Wells Fantasy

A newspaper cutting of the incident

The broadcast returned to the music of Ramon Raquello, but soon it was interrupted again with more news. Now a strange meteor had fallen to earth, impacting violently on a farm near Grovers Mill, New Jersey. A reporter was soon on hand to describe the eerie scene around the meteor crater, and the broadcast switched over to continuous coverage of this rapidly unfolding event.

To the dismay of the terrified radio audience, the events around the Grovers Mill meteor crater rapidly escalated from the merely strange to the positively ominous. It turned out that the meteor was not a meteor. It was, in fact, a spaceship, out of which a tentacled creature, presumably a Martian, emerged and blasted the onlookers with a deadly heat-ray.

The Martian sunk back into the crater, but reemerged soon afterwards housed inside a gigantic, three-legged death machine. The Martian quickly disposed of 7,000 armed soldiers surrounding the crater, and then it began marching across the landscape, joined by other Martians. The Martian invaders blasted people and communication lines with their heat-rays, while simultaneously releasing a toxic black gas against which gas masks proved useless.

Believing that the nation had been invaded by Martians, many listeners panicked. Some people loaded blankets and supplies in their cars and prepared to flee. One mother in New England reportedly packed her babies and lots of bread into a car, figuring that "if everything is burning, you can't eat money, but you can eat bread." Other people hid in cellars, hoping that the poisonous gas would blow over them. One college senior drove forty-five miles at breakneck speed in a valiant attempt to save his girlfriend.

By the time the night was over, however, almost all of these people had learned that the news broadcast was entirely fictitious. It was simply the weekly broadcast of Orson Welles and the Mercury Theatre. That week, in honour of Halloween, they had decided to stage a highly dramatized and updated version of H.G. Wells' story, *The War of the Worlds*.

The broadcast reached a huge audience, demonstrating the enormous reach of radio at that time. Approximately six million people heard it. Out of this number it was long thought that almost one million people panicked. More recent research, however, suggests that the number of people who panicked is probably far lower. In fact, some skeptics contend that the idea that the broadcast touched off a huge national scare is more of a hoax than the broadcast itself, which was never intended to fool anyone. (At four separate points during the broadcast, including the beginning, it was clearly stated that what people were hearing was a play.)

The idea that hundreds of thousands of people panicked may have arisen because the media exaggerated the figures in order to dramatize the panic.

Despite the contention that the panic may not have been as widespread as originally thought, many people undeniably did panic. What might have caused them to believe that the broadcast was real?

First, many people tuned in late and missed the announcement made at the beginning of the broadcast that what followed was merely a staged dramatization. By the time a second disclaimer was made, the most alarming portion of the play had already been broadcast.

Second, the global situation in 1938 provided a context that allowed many to believe such a series of events could be unfolding. Tensions in Europe were rising, and it had been very common during the previous three months for radio broadcasts to be interrupted by reporters delivering ominous news from Europe. Many who panicked later explained they had assumed the Martian invasion was a cleverly disguised German attack.

Most of those who panicked were middle-aged or older. Younger listeners tended not to panic because they recognized Orson Welles's voice as the voice of the hero in the popular radio series, *The Shadow*.

The 1938 broadcast was not the only time a dramatized broadcast of H.G. Wells' *War of the Worlds* was mistaken for an account of real events. In November 1944 the play caused a similar panic when it was broadcast in Santiago, Chile, and in February 1949 it once again stirred up unrest when it was performed by a radio station in Quito, Ecuador. The situation in Ecuador provoked an angry mob to surround the radio station and burn it to the ground.

Naked Came the Stranger

In 1969, Newsday's Mike McGrady conspired with twenty-three fellow writers and literature critics to produce a work that reflected the poorly written texts that were quickly becoming favourites among American audiences. Each of the contributors penned a single chapter and combined them together under the title, "*Naked Came the Stranger*", with the writing credit given to imaginary author 'Penelope Ashe.' The book describes the erotic adventures of Gillian Blake, following the discovery of her husband's infidelity. For publicity purposes, McGrady's sister-in-law acted as Penelope Ashe, thereby furthering the hoax's execution.

The book

The book quickly became a widespread hit, earning itself the number one spot on the *New York Times* Bestseller list for a week. The authors, having each made a good-deal of money from the book's sales, eventually decided to expose the hoax on the David Frost Show, thereby ending the ruse. The book continued to sell, and was eventually adapted into a pornographic film of the same name.

50 Operation Mincemeat

In 1943 the body of a British officer, Major William Martin, was discovered off the coast of Spain, near Huelva. British diplomats strongly requested that all documents found with the body be returned to them, and the Spanish government eventually complied. But upon examination, it was obvious the documents had been opened and read before their return. This was exactly what the British had hoped would happen, because Major Martin did not exist. He was part of a military hoax, codenamed Operation Mincemeat, designed to fool the Germans.

The Operation Mincemeat team

The British military had obtained a cadaver, chained a briefcase containing supposedly top-secret papers to its wrist, and dropped it in the sea off the coast of Spain. The plan was that the Germans, via the Spanish, would find the body and read the fake papers. The papers stated that the Allies' planned invasion of southern Europe would begin with an attack on Greece and Sardinia. In reality, the Allies planned to attack Sicily first. The hoax was successful.

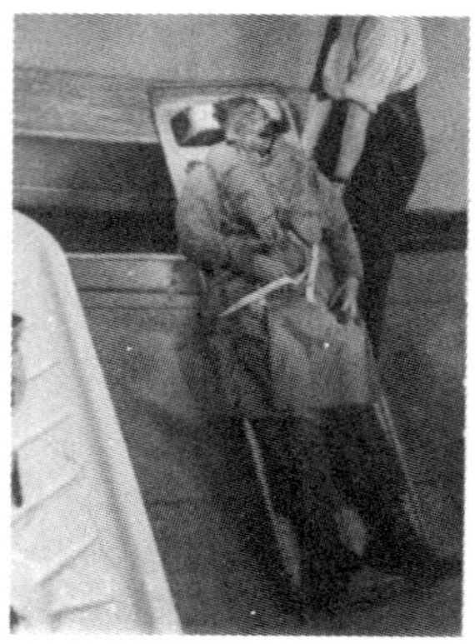

Body of a British officer was discovered off the coast of Spain

When the Allies launched their offensive on Sicily, most of the heavy German equipment had been moved to defend these other locations.

Ewen Montagu, the British officer who devised the operation, later wrote a book about it titled *The Man Who Never Was*. The book was subsequently made into a movie.

OO

BANG

51 The Accidental Time Traveller - Rudolph Fentz

The story of Rudolph Fentz was for many decades considered to be an unsolved mystery, as well as a case of possible time travel. According to the story, in June 1950 a man suddenly appeared in the centre of New York City's Times Square, as if from out of the blue. He was wearing old-fashioned clothes and sported the kind of mutton-chop sideburns that had gone out of fashion decades ago. Glancing about himself, a look first of astonishment and then of panic flashed across his face. He began to sprint forwards, and was then struck down and killed by a car.

When police examined the man, they found nineteenth-century money in his pockets as well as business cards identifying him as Rudolph Fentz. But they couldn't locate records of a man named Fentz anywhere until they came across the old widow of a Rudolph Fentz Jr. The widow told them that her father-in-law, Rudolph Fentz Sr., had disappeared one day without a trace in 1876. Intriguingly, the address of her father-in-law matched the address on the mysterious stranger's business cards. So the police were left with an enigma. Rudolph Fentz appeared to have vanished in 1876, only to reappear in 1950. Had he somehow fallen into a time-hole that had sucked him seventy-four years through time?

For decades this tale was popular among members of Europe's paranormal research community, and it was generally accepted as true – an example of a genuine mystery – until 2005 when researcher Chris Aubeck investigated its history.

Aubeck discovered that the tale had begun life as a science-fiction story penned by Jack Finney and published in a 1951 anthology. Two years later a writer named Ralph Holland reprinted the story in a booklet, but he did so without permission and removed all indication that the story was fiction. Holland was a member of a group called Borderland that was committed to promoting belief in the existence of a 'fourth dimension.' The Fentz story, when presented as fact, ably served this agenda. Through Holland's booklet, the tale of the accidental time traveller made its way to Europe, where it soon took root and circulated for decades within the European paranormal research community.

The Zeuglodon

It looked like a sea serpent. It swam like a sea serpent. Its original name, Basilosaurus, even meant King of Reptiles. But was the Zeuglodon, an aquatic animal that apparently lived from 37 to 53 million years ago, a sea serpent?

In 1845 Albert Koch, owner of a small museum in St. Louis, set out to visit Alabama. He heard rumours that people were finding the bones of sea serpents in the ground.

Koch was no stranger to paleontology. He had already dug up the bones of a giant mastodon and took it on a tour of America. Koch, more a huckster than a serious scientist, had added an extra ten vertebrae from another skeleton and wooden blocks to make the creature look even more gigantic than it really was. In 1842 he sold it to The British Museum, who shrunk the creature back to normal size before putting it on display.

Arriving in Alabama, Koch found these "sea serpent" vertebrae so common that people were using them for furniture. Finding a full skeleton was more difficult, and it took him months to discover a nearly complete set of bones near the Sintabogure River. It took three more months of hard work to excavate the bones and pack them into five wagonloads. These Koch, using his old tricks, assembled into a skeleton 114 feet long using the vertebrae of five different animals.

Koch took his creation on tour. In New York the newspaper *The New York Disector* reviewed the exhibit: "The serpent of the Deucalion deluge, slain by Apollo Pythius, is beheld with scarcely the aid of the dullest fancy."

The creature was christened Hydroargos sillimani by Koch, which meant "Silliman's Master-of-the-Seas." Benjamin Silliman, a professor at Yale University, had been open to the possibility that

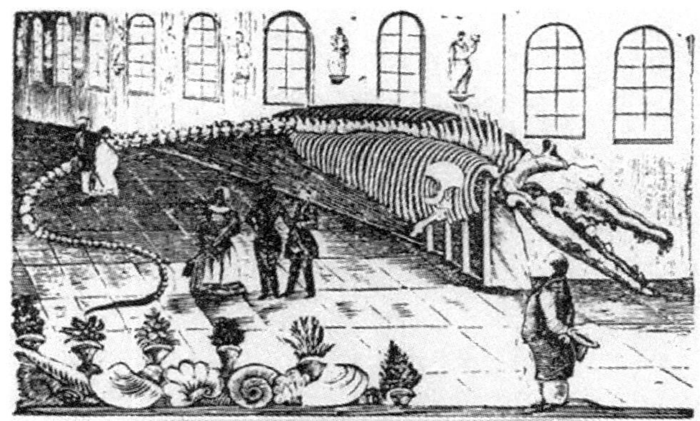

The Zeuglodon

sea serpents might exist after some sightings in New England in 1827. Silliman, not wishing to be associated with Koch's creation, however, demanded the name be changed and Koch complied.

Koch would eventually take his monster to Europe, sell it, return to Alabama, excavate another and take it on tour also. But was what he was showing really an exaggerated sea serpent?

A few years before in 1832, a box arrived at the American Philosophical Society in Philadelphia. In it was a lump of rock and a letter from one Judge Bry of Louisiana. The lump was the fossil of what Bry believed might be a sea monster. The fossil was given to Dr. Richard Harlan, a surgeon and paleontologist, to examine. He thought it might have come from a sea going-lizard. More bones from the same type of creature arrived from Alabama including a jaw. The jaw was hollow which seemed to support Harlan's reptile theory, so the creature was christened the Basilosaurus which meant King of Reptiles making it a true "sea serpent." Harlan did this even though the creature had teeth that were narrow toward the front of the jaw, but larger toward the back, normally characteristic of a mammal.

In 1839 Harlan traveled to London to address a meeting of the Geographic Society. When he arrived he was plunged into a controversy between scientists who believed that mammals lived during the Mesozoic Period and those that didn't. Even though the

Basilosaurus was from the following period, the Eocene, it might prove that some non-identical teeth, found in Mesozoic jaws, could belong to a form of reptile, instead of mammals.

In London the great English anatomist, Richard Owen (who coined the term dinosaur a few years later), got a hold of Harlan's fossils and began a close examination. He noted that the hollow jaw was not just characteristic of reptiles, but was found on the sperm whale, too. He also discovered that the shape of the spinal cord channel in the vertebrae was like that of a whale's, not a reptile. Finally by splitting open some of the teeth, Owen showed that they were more like a marine mammal than that of a marine lizard. Harlan had to agree and the Basilosaurus ceased to be a sea serpent, but was instead reclassified as a primitive form of whale.

Skeletons of the Zeuglodon have been found across North America and in parts of Africa. In life the creatures ranged from fifty-five to seventy-five feet long and sometimes had skull a five feet in length. It has the remains of hind leg bones suggesting that the animal's ancestors once lived on the land (Scientists believe that all whales came from a four footed hyena-like creature known as a Mesonychid).

There has been speculation that the Zeuglodon is not dead, but inhabiting cold water lakes like Loch Ness and Lake Champlain as their famous monsters. While this seems unlikely, it is not at all impossible, since the Coelacanth, a primitive fish thought to be extinct for 65 million years, showed up off the coast of South Africa in 1938.

The Zeuglodon is the official state fossil of Alabama and is protected by law. So if you find one on your next visit to that southern state, make sure you call the governor and ask permission before you take him home with you.

OO

53 Elmyr de Hory – Con Man

In 1955, Harvard University's Fogg Museum bought a Matisse drawing, "A Lady with Flowers and Pomegranates," from a Miami art dealer named E. Raynal. Raynal also agreed to lend the Fogg additional drawings from his collection, including two Modiglianis, a Renoir, and a second Matisse. The Museum's curator Agnes Mongan examined these drawings and determined that the Renoir and the Modiglianis weren't authentic.

Elmyr de Hory

The Fogg Museum's assistant curator Emily Rauh followed up to determine the authenticity of the Matisse drawings. She contacted other Matisse collectors around the country. A Miami collector told her that 'E. Raynal' was actually in possession of hundreds of Matisse drawings. This raised even more suspicion.

After receiving photographs of Matisse drawings from collectors, dealers, and other museums, Rauh closely compared and examined the works for authenticity. On further investigation, 'Raynal'□ himself was discovered to be a fake. In truth, he was a Hungarian expatriate named Elmyr de Hory whose other pseudonyms included 'von Houry', 'Herzog', 'Cassou', 'Hoffman', and 'Dory-Boutin.'

Elmyr de Hory's career as an art forger began in post-war Paris. As a struggling artist, he couldn't sell his own work, so he created his first fake, a Picasso that he easily sold to a wealthy English friend, Lady Malcolm Campbell. Seeing such immediate success, de Hory began imitating other artists including Matisse, Dufy, Derain, and Renoir. Along the way, he gathered a team of shady confederates. They posed as art dealers on four continents, selling de Hory's bogus masterpieces for huge profits.

In the sixties, de Hory's base of operations was in Spain on the island of Ibiza. In 1969, author Clifford Irving's book '*Fake!*' told de Hory's story.

Years later, Irving himself would be exposed as a con man after selling a fake Howard Hughes autobiography to a publisher.

In 1975, Orson Welles directed the documentary 'F is for Fake' featuring both de Hory and Clifford Irving.

After being exposed, Elmyr de Hory kept producing his fakes, but signed his own name on the back.

In 1976, de Hory committed suicide before facing extradition to France to face fraud charges. To this day, some known de Hory paintings and drawings (with his signature on the back) continue to sell, some for close to the same prices as the real Picassos, Modiglianis, and Derains.

The Real Rampa

The Third Eye, by Tuesday Lobsang Rampa, was first published in 1956. It purported to be his autobiographical account of growing up in Tibet and studying Tibetan Buddhism.

Rampa claimed he had been born into a wealthy Tibetan family and at the age of seven had joined the Chakpori Lamasery in Lhasa where he studied medicine, astrology, Tibetan history, telepathy, hypnotism, and the theory of reincarnation. He also underwent a painful operation to open up the "third eye" in the middle of his forehead. This operation had bestowed upon him amazing psychic powers.

Rampa's book sold well, but soon questions began to be raised about his identity. People wondered why he spoke English like a native-born speaker if he had, as he claimed, learned the language in a Japanese prisoner-of-war camp. Scholars also pointed out numerous errors in his book. For instance, they noted that in Tibetan culture the "third eye" was understood to be a psychical centre that was supposed to be opened by meditation, never by surgery.

Keen to debunk what he was sure was a fraud, the Tibetologist Heinrich Harrer hired a private detective, Clifford Burgess, to determine the validity of Rampa's tale.

Burgess published the results of his investigation in February, 1958 in the *Daily Mail*. He revealed that Rampa had never been to Tibet, nor had he ever had any operation done to his forehead. Instead Rampa was actually Cyril Henry Hoskins, born in Devon, England, and son of a plumber. He had worked first as an assistant to his father, then as an employee of a surgical-implements firm, and later as a clerk in a correspondence school.

Rampa

But Cyril, it turned out, had always been interested in the study of the occult. He had studied it as much as he could in his spare time. And one day he had taken his interest a step further by growing a beard, shaving his head, and changing his name to "Dr. Kuan-suo." He later changed it again to Tuesday Lobsang Rampa.

When his true identity was exposed, Hoskins was initially nowhere to be found. But reporters eventually tracked him down to Ireland, where he said he was too ill to receive visitors. Eventually he offered an explanation for his dual identity. He said that it was true he was born Cyril Henry Hoskins, but that the soul of Rampa had transmigrated into his body. Therefore, according to him, all the information in his book was true.

Despite having been proven to be a phony – a plumber's son posing as a Tibetan monk – a market still existed for Rampa's writings. So he continued on with his career as Tuesday Lobsang Rampa, authoring numerous books before his death in 1981. However, none of them sold as well as *The Third Eye.*

OO

55 The Book of Mormon

The Book of Mormon is considered by the Church of Jesus Christ of Latter Day Saints to be a divinely inspired book of equal value to the Bible. Joseph Smith, founder of the Mormon religion, claimed that he was directed by an Angel to a hill near his home in which he found golden tablets containing the full text of the book. With the books he found two objects called the Urim and Thummim which he described as a pair of crystals joined in the form of a large pair of spectacles. Unfortunately, after Smith finished his translation, he had to return the tablets to the Angel, so there is no physical evidence that they ever existed.

Joseph Smith

The book refers to a group of Jews that moved to and settled in America where Jesus visited them. Some segments of the Book of Mormon contain sections copied directly from the King James version of the Bible – the Bible that was most popular at the time and used by Joseph Smith. One example is Mark 16:15-18 which is quoted nearly word-for-word in Mormon 9:22-24. In addition, the book mimics the literary and linguistic style of the King James Bible. Linguistic experts have stated that the entire book is written by one man, and is not written by a combination of authors (the prophets as claimed by Smith). Additionally, the book refers to animals and crops that did not exist in America until Columbus arrived: ass, bull, calf, cattle, cow, domestic goat, horse, ox, domestic sheep, sow, swine, elephants, wheat, and barley.

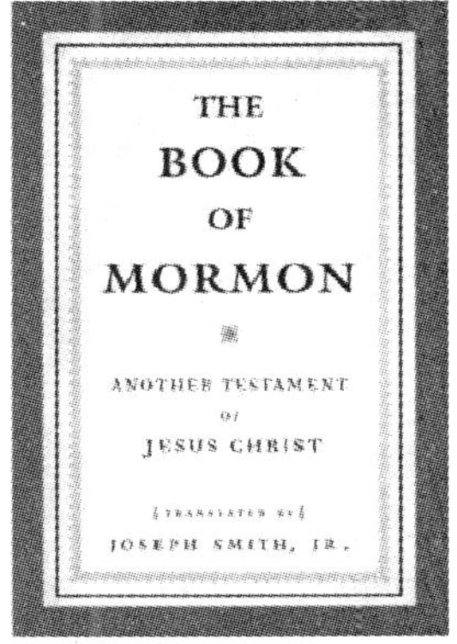

The Book of Mormon

The most compelling proof that Joseph Smith was perpetuating a fraud is the Book of Abraham. In 1835 Smith was able to use his Urim and Thummim to translate some Egyptian scrolls that he was given access to (at that time no one could read hieroglyphics). Upon inspection, Smith declared that they contained the Book of Abraham. He promptly translated the lot and it was accepted as scripture by the church. The scrolls vanished and everyone thought the story would end there. But it didn't – in 1966 the original scrolls were found in the New York Metropolitan Museum of Art. The scrolls turned out to be a standard Egyptian text that was often buried with the dead. To this day the Book of Abraham is a source of discomfort for the Mormon religion.

56 The Autobiography of Howard Hughes

Throughout history there are numerous cases of forgers faking diaries and biographies of people who are already dead. But, for obvious reasons, it is far less common for a forger to fake the biography of a person who is still alive. But this is exactly what happened when writer Clifford Irving forged the "autobiography" of the eccentric billionaire Howard Hughes, while Hughes was still alive.

Clifford Irving

Hughes had retreated from public life in 1958, thereafter refusing to be photographed or interviewed. This behavior created an enormous amount of speculation and curiosity about his life. Publishers were eager to publish the inside story of how Hughes spent his days, knowing such a book would be an instant bestseller. But unfortunately neither Hughes nor any of his closest associates were talking. Until Irving came along, that is.

In 1971 Irving told his publisher, McGraw-Hill, that Hughes had contacted him after reading and enjoying one of his earlier books. Hughes, he said, wanted to write an autobiography in order to set straight all the lies and rumours that were circulating about his life, and he wanted Irving to ghostwrite the work. Irving produced letters from Hughes (all forged) to prove the offer was real. McGraw-Hill completely fell for Irving's story. They eventually gave him almost $1,000,000 in order to secure the rights to the work, and in return Irving handed them Hughes's "autobiography" a few months later.

Howard Hughes

The scheme almost worked, until something happened that Irving hadn't counted on. Hughes broke his long media silence in order to come forward and publicly deny all knowledge of Irving and the autobiography.

After returning the money he had taken, Irving spent a short time in jail. When he got out he wrote the true account of how he had almost gotten away with writing the fake autobiography of Howard Hughes. The fake autobiography itself never saw the light of day until it was published on the internet in 1999.

A 2006 movie, *The Hoax*, starring Richard Gere, tells the story of Irving's almost successful con.

OO

The Piltdown Chicken

The National Geographic Society held a press conference on October 15, 1999 to announce a major discovery: It had found a 125-million-year-old fossil in northeastern China that appeared to be the long-sought missing link between dinosaurs and birds. For over twenty years paleontologists had debated whether birds were descended from dinosaurs. This fossil seemed to provide conclusive proof they were.

SEATTLE, WASHINGTON • EAST SIDE JOURNAL - 01/22/2000 pg A5

PILTDOWN CHICKEN

The finding was initially trumpeted as the missing link that proved birds evolved from dinosaurs. In 1999 a fossil smuggled out of China allegedly showing a dinosaur with birdlike plumage was displayed triumphantly at the National Geographic Society and written up in the society's November magazine. Paleontologists were abuzz. Unfortunately, like the hominid skull with an ape jaw discovered in the Piltdown quarries of England in 1912, the whole thing turned out to be a hoax. The fossil apparently was the flight of fancy of a Chinese farmer who had rigged together bird bits and a meat-eater's tail.

DISCOVER • Oct. 2000

This model reconstruction of an Archaeoraptor liaoningensis fossil is hailed by some scientists as an important find for the theory that birds'evolved from dinosaurs. An eminent paleontologist in Beijing, however, says what was found is really a composite of fossils from different creatures, and is not the evolutionary link some thought it was.

Scientist disputes fossil's link between dinosaurs and birds

Paleontologist says creature actually is a composite of fossils

By Elaine Kurtenbach
Associated Press

BEIJING — A fossil hailed as an important find for the theory that birds evolved from dinosaurs is really a composite of fossils from different creatures, a Chinese scientist says.

Xu Xing, an eminent paleontologist in Beijing, said he has found fossils that prove the fossilized turkey-sized creature unveiled last year may not be the evolutionary link some thought it was.

Xu's claim has forced paleontology circles, which greeted the find with some fanfare, to take a second look. And the controversy has highlighted the pitfalls of international research projects involving fossils that are often smuggled out of China and sold overseas.

Scientists have other evidence that birds evolved from dinosaurs, and Xu's finding doesn't overturn the theory.

The National Geographic Society convened a press conference in October to announce the discovery of the dinosaur, dubbed Archaeoraptor liaoningensis, which lived 120 million to 140 million years ago.

Unlike feathered dinosaurs discovered earlier, the Archaeoraptor showed evidence that it could fly, they said.

The Archaeoraptor fossil, however, included specimens that had been smuggled out of China and thus are of uncertain provenance.

Now National Geographic magazine plans to publish a note in its March issue saying that CT scans of the fossil appeared to confirm Xu's observations and had "revealed anomalies" in the reconstruction, said National Geographic Society spokeswoman Barbara Moffet. She added that more information was needed.

Xu contends the Archaeoraptor is a combination of two fossils: one of the body and head of a birdlike creature and the other of the tail of a different dinosaur. He said he has found another fossil, in a private collection in China, that contains the mirror image of the supposed tail of the Archaeoraptor.

Fossils often break in two when the rocks containing them are split in excavation.

"This is a completely new dinosaur. It's nothing like the Archaeoraptor," Xu, of China's Institute of Vertebrate Paleontology and Paleoanthropology, said in an interview.

Paleontologist Stephen Czerkas, who bought the Archaeoraptor fossil at a gem and mineral sale in Utah, said Xu may be right.

"No one has been able to actually compare the two fossils side-by-side. Research is still ongoing. But that is what we are all tending to believe."

Still, Czerkas said the Archaeoraptor, even without its tail, remained a very important find.

"It's still totally one of a kind, first time anyone has seen anything like this before," said Czerkas, who with his wife, Sylvia, runs the Dinosaur Museum in Blanding, Utah.

He said Xu's dinosaur, a dromaeosaur that could not fly, was also "very exciting."

"We've never had a tail with feathers," Czerkas said. "We're getting new information about the dromaeosaur we've never had before."

Xu said he could not disclose further details about his find until he finished a research article for Nature magazine to be published later this year. He has invited U.S. scientists to visit Beijing to examine his find.

The fossils were unearthed in western Liaoning province, a barren, semi-desert region about 260 miles northeast of Beijing that is a treasure trove for paleontologists.

"Lots of specimens have been smuggled out for commercial purposes," Xu said. "For science, this is a disaster.

"When pieces are stolen and smuggled out, sometimes blocks of fossils are matched together mistakenly. That can be a big mistake, and it misleads the public."

"NOT" IT'S A MISSING LINK

NATIONAL GEOGRAPHIC NOVEMBER 1999

A news paper cutting of the hoax

In addition to the press conference, held at the National Geographic's corporate headquarters, the Society simultaneously published a glossy article about the find in its well-known magazine.

The fossil bird, when living, would have been about the size of a large chicken, or a turkey. But it would have been a turkey that bore the long tail of a dinosaur. It was this mixture of dinosaur and bird parts that made researchers believe they had found the dinosaur-bird missing link. As Christopher Sloan, author of the National Geographic article, enthusiastically wrote, "Its long arms and small body scream 'Bird!' Its long, stiff tail... screams 'Dinosaur!'"

What Sloan didn't realize at the time, was that the body and tail together should have screamed 'Fake!'

Xu Xing, a Chinese scientist who had initially helped to identify the fossil, eventually realized it was a fraud when he found a second fossil containing an exact, mirror-image duplicate of the Archaeoraptor's tail, but attached to a different body. Fossil stones, when taken from the ground, often cleave in two, producing two mirror-image sets of fossil slabs. Evidently someone had taken one of the slabs bearing the tail fossil and affixed it to a fossil of a bird, thereby producing a hybrid dinosaur-bird creature.

National Geographic published an admission of its mistake in March 2000 and a fuller analysis of how it had been duped in October of that year. It admitted red flags had been raised about the discovery at various points, but that it had failed to see them. More seriously, it acknowledged rushing its find into publication before more scholarly journals had the chance to peer-review the data.

U.S. News & World Report was the first to refer to the Archaeoraptor Liaoningensis forgery as the case of the Piltdown Chicken, alluding to the infamous Piltdown Man hoax of 1912.

OO

58 Name: Samukeliso Sithole, Sex: ??

Samukeliso Sithole was a rising female star in the world of Zimbabwe athletics. The 17-year-old track-and-field athlete had won awards at various regional athletic events, including five gold medals at the Southern Region Youth Championship in 2004. But in 2005 her career came to an abrupt halt when it was revealed that 'she' was actually a 'he'.

Samukeliso Sithole

Sithole's secret was exposed in January 2005 by a female friend, Melita Mudondiro, who felt her dignity had been violated after she had undressed in front of him, believing he was a woman. Sithole's uncle, Dryton Mkandla, later informed Mudondiro of Sithole's true gender, and she decided to file criminal charges against him.

A doctor's report confirmed that Sithole was male.

At the subsequent trial, Sithole offered an unusual defense to explain the deception. He explained he had been born with both male and female organs. His parents had then consulted a traditional Chipinge healer who had used a mixture of herbs to make his male organs disappear, turning him into a female.

However, Sithole's parents had apparently failed to pay the healer the full bill for these services. As a result, the healer took revenge by causing Sithole's male genitals to grow back. Sithole assured the court that, if he would be able to pay the healer the remainder of the balance, his male organs would again disappear and he would revert to being a female.

Further investigation revealed that Samukeliso Sithole was not the athlete's real name. He had been born as either Fadzai Fuzani or Mduduzi Ngwenya (reports vary). But one of his teachers at the Ndllamatuli Secondary School in Silobela helped him to obtain the birth certificate of Samukeliso Sithole, who was a female student at the same school. With this birth certificate, he was able to obtain a national registration card, which allowed him to compete in athletic events as a woman.

The court sentenced Sithole (aka Fuzani or Ngwenya) to three-and-a-half years in prison for impersonating a woman and offending the dignity of the female athlete who undressed in front of him.

59 The Priory of Sion

The Priory of Sion has been characterized as anything from the most influential secret society in Western history to a modern Rosicrucian-esque group, but, ultimately, has been shown to be a hoax created in 1956 by Pierre Plantard, a pretender to the French throne. The evidence presented in support of its historical existence is not considered authentic or persuasive by established historians, academics, and universities, and the evidence was later discovered to have been forged and then planted in various locations around France by Plantard and his associates.

Pierre Plantard with his son

Between 1961 and 1984 Plantard contrived a mythical pedigree of the Priory of Sion claiming that it was the offshoot of the monastic order housed in the Abbey of Sion, which had been founded in the Kingdom of Jerusalem during the First Crusade and later absorbed by the Jesuits in 1617. Plantard hoped that the Priory of Sion would become an influential cryptopolitical irregular masonic lodge dedicated to the restoration of chivalry and monarchy, which would promote Plantard's own claim to the throne of France.

The priory recently gained interest again (despite easily obtainable proof that it is a fake) through the publication of the book *The Da Vinci Code* which the author, Dan Brown, claims to be fact (proving that he lied outright about his alleged years of research for the book).

OO

60 Stolen: Mona Lisa Hoax

It was a quiet, humid Monday morning in Paris, 21 August 1911. Three men were hurrying out of the Louvre. It was odd, since the museum was closed to visitors on Mondays, and odder still with what one of them had under his jacket.

They were Vincenzo Perugia and the brothers Lancelotti, Vincenzo and Michele, young Italian handymen. They had come to the Louvre on Sunday afternoon and secreted themselves overnight in a narrow storeroom near the Salon Carré, a gallery stuffed with Renaissance paintings. In the morning, wearing white workmen's smocks, they had gone into the Salon Carré. They seized a small painting off the wall. Quickly, they ripped off its glass shadow box and frame and Perugia hid it under his clothes. They slipped out of the gallery, down a back stairwell and through a side entrance and into the streets of Paris.

Mona Lisa

They had stolen the Mona Lisa.

It would be 26 hours before someone noticed that the painting was missing. It was understandable. At the time the Louvre was the largest building in the world, with more than 1,000 rooms spread over 45 acres. Security was weak; fewer than 150 guards protected the quarter-of-a-million objects. Statues disappeared, paintings got damaged. (A heavy statue of the Egyptian god Isis was stolen about a year before the Mona Lisa and in 1907, a woman was sentenced to six months in prison for slashing Jean Auguste Ingres' Pius VII in the Sistine Chapel.)

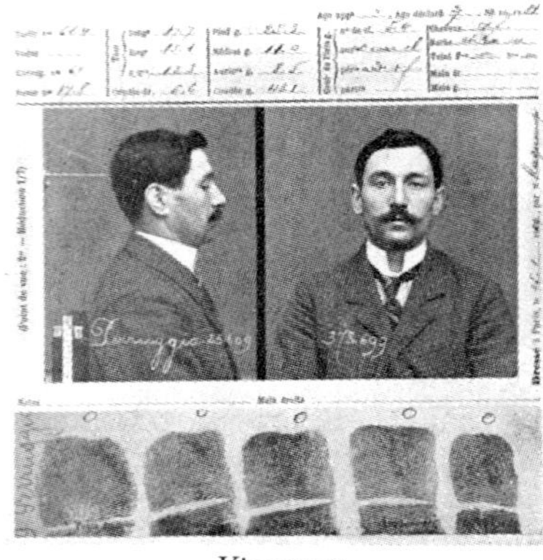

Vincenzo

At the time of the "Mona Lisa" heist, Leonardo da Vinci's masterpiece was far from the most visited item in the museum. Leonardo painted the portrait around 1507, and it was not until the 1860s that art critics claimed the Mona Lisa was one of the finest examples of Renaissance painting. This judgment, however, had not yet filtered beyond a thin slice of the intelligentsia, and interest in it was relatively minimal. In his 1878 guidebook to Paris, travel writer Karl Baedeker offered a paragraph of description about the portrait; in 1907 he had a mere two sentences, much less than the other gems in the museum, such as Nike of Samothrace and Venus de Milo.

Which isn't to say it was obscure. A letter mailed to the Louvre in 1910 from Vienna had threatened the Mona Lisa so museum officials hired the glazier firm Cobier to put a dozen of its more prized paintings under glass. The work took three months; one of the Cobier men assigned to the project was Vincenzo Perugia. The son of a bricklayer, Perugia grew up in Dumenza, a Lombardy village north of Milan. In 1907 at the age of 25, Vincenzo left home, trying out Paris, Milan and then Lyon. After a year, he settled in Paris with his two brothers in the Italian enclave in the 10th Arrondissement.

Perugia was short, just 5 feet 3, and quick to challenge any insult, to himself or his nation. His brothers called him a passoide o megloi, a nut or madman. His fellow French construction workers, Perugia later testified in court, "almost always called me 'mangia maccheroni' [macaroni eater] and very often they stole my personal property and salted my wine."

Twice the Parisian police arrested Perugia. In June 1908 he spent a night in jail for attempting to rob a prostitute. Eight months later, he clocked in a week in the Macon, the notorious Parisian prison and paid a 16-franc fine for carrying a gun during a fistfight. He even quarreled with his future co-conspirators; he once stopped speaking to Vincenzo Lancelotti over a disputed 1-franc loan.

Perugia wanted to be more than a construction worker. Appearing in court in 1914 for the theft of the Mona Lisa, he was called a housepainter by the prosecution. Perugia stood up and declared himself a pittore, an artist. He had taught himself how to read and sometimes holed himself up in coffeehouses or museums, poring through books and newspapers.

Stealing the Mona Lisa made sense. Most purloined paintings that were not immediately held for ransom didn't go to a wealthy aristocrat's secret hideaway, but instead slide into an illicit pipeline being used as barter or collateral for drugs, arms and other stolen goods. Perugia had enough connections to criminal circles that he hoped to barter or sell it.

Unfortunately for Perugia, the Mona Lisa got too hot to hock. Initially, the afternoon newspapers in Paris had nothing on Monday, and the following morning's papers were also curiously quiet on the matter. Would the Louvre cover it up, pretend it had not happened?

Finally, late on Tuesday, there was a media explosion when the Louvre issued a statement announcing the theft. Newspapers around the world came out with banner headlines. Wanted posters for the painting appeared on Parisian walls. Crowds massed at police headquarters. Thousands of spectators, including Franz Kafka, flooded into the Salon Carré when the Louvre reopened after a week to stare at the empty wall with its four lonely iron hooks. Kafka and his traveling companion Max Brod marveled at the "mark of shame" at the Louvre and attended a vaudeville show lampooning the theft.

Satirical postcards, a short film and cabaret songs followed – popular culture seized upon the theft and turned high art into mass art. Perugia realized that he had not pinched an old Italian painting from a decaying royal palace. He had unluckily stolen what had become, in a few short days, the world's most famous painting.

Perugia squirreled the Mona Lisa away in the false bottom of a wooden trunk in his room at his boardinghouse. When the Parisian police interrogated him in November 1911 as a part of their interviews of all Louvre employees, he blithely said he only learned of the theft from the newspapers and that the reason he was late to work that Monday in August – as his employer had told the police – was that he had drunk too much the night before and overslept.

The police bought the story. Supremely inept, they ignored Perugia and instead arrested the artist Pablo Picasso and the poet and critic Guillaume Apollinaire. (They were friends with a thief who admitted to pinching little sculptures from the Louvre.) The two were promptly released.

In December 1913, after 28 months, Perugia left his Parisian boardinghouse with his trunk and took a train to Florence where he tried to offload the painting on an art dealer who promptly called the police. Perugia was arrested. After a brief trial in Florence, he pleaded guilty and served only eight months in prison.

Thanks to the high-profile heist, the Mona Lisa was now a global icon. Under a shower of even more publicity, it returned to the Louvre following mobbed exhibitions in Florence, Milan and Rome. In the first two days after it was rehung in the Salon Carré, more than 100,000 people viewed it. Today, eight million people see the Mona Lisa every year.

As soon as the painting was stolen in 1911, conspiracy theories sprouted up. Was it a hoax? Some said the theft was the French government's way of trying to distract public opinion from uprisings in colonial West Africa. A few months before the painting was found, the *New York Times* speculated that Louvre restorers had botched a restoration job of the Mona Lisa; to cover this up, the museum concocted the story of an outlandish theft.

Even after the recovery of the Mona Lisa, the world was still incredulous. How could a few Italian carpenters have pulled this caper off by themselves? For years, rumours surfaced that a gang of international art thieves had poached the painting and

Mona Lisa recovered

substituted a fake that was in Perugia's possession when he was caught in Florence. In a 1932 issue of *The Saturday Evening Post*, Karl Decker, an American journalist, offered a twist: a shady Argentine swindler had arranged for six copies of the Mona Lisa to be made and sold after Perugia's theft (each buyer thought he had the original).

Two English-language nonfiction accounts of the theft, a 1981 book by Seymour Reit and a 2009 retelling by R.A. Scotti, carry Decker's story to the hilt, even though there is no supporting historical evidence.

A century has passed since Perugia pinched the painting, and yet historians are still reluctant to give him the credit as the unwitting catalyst for making the Mona Lisa the world-famous icon that it is today.

OO

61 The Protocols of the Elders of Zion

The Protocol of the Elders of Zion is a text that purports to describe a Jewish and Masonic plot to achieve world domination. It is one of the most well-known and discussed examples of literary forgery. Numerous independent investigations have concluded it to be either a plagiarism or a hoax. The Protocols is widely considered to be the beginning of contemporary conspiracy theory literature, and takes the form of an instruction manual to a new member of the "elders," describing how they will run the world through control of the media and finance, and replace the traditional social order with one based on mass manipulation.

The Protocols of the Elders of Zion

Continued usage of the Protocols as an antisemitic propaganda tool substantially diminished with the defeat of the Nazis in World War II. It is still frequently quoted and reprinted by some anti-Semitic circles, and is sometimes used as evidence of an alleged Jewish cabal, especially in the Middle East. Elements of the text in the Protocols appears to be plagiarized from an 1864 pamphlet, *Dialogue in Hell Between Machiavelli and Montesquieu*, written by the French satirist Maurice Joly. Joly's work attacks the political ambitions of Napoleon III using Machiavelli as a diabolical plotter in Hell as a stand-in for Napoleon's views.

Maurice Joly and his book "The Dialogue in Hell Between Machiavelli and Montesquieu"

Interestingly, many of the protocols aims have been achieved. For example: Universal suffrage, wide acceptance of pornography, the spread of Darwinism, Socialism, and Materialism.